THE GUIDE TO GOLD PANNING

N. L. BARLEE

ISBN 0-88839-986-3

First Printing .... July 1972
Second Printing .... June 1973
Third Printing .... July 1974
Fourth Printing .... July 1975
Fifth Printing .... July 1976
Sixth Printing .... July 1977
Seventh Printing .... March 1979
Second Edition, First Printing .... June 1979
Second Edition, Second Printing .... March 1980
Third Edition, First Printing .... May 1984

ACKNOWLEDGEMENTS

Many of the photographs in this book are from the Provincial Archives in Victoria. The others are from private sources and individuals.

Cover photos courtesy of the Ministry of Tourism.

Printed in Hong Kong

Published simultaneously in Canada and the United States by

HANCOCK HOUSE PUBLISHERS LTD.
19313 Zero Ave., Surrey, B.C. V3S 5J9
HANCOCK HOUSE PUBLISHERS INC.
1431 Harrison Avenue, Blaine, WA 98230

CONTENTS

FOREWORD

Of all the provinces in Canada, British Columbia is the only one where there are innumerable placer gold creeks which can still be worked by prospectors with occasional surprising results.

There is something compelling about prospecting for gold. The lure of panning for the royal metal and the companionship of a gold stream are a unique and memorable combination - one which has attracted and held countless numbers of individuals fascinated for years.

It is not difficult to visualize the gold rushes of the past when names likes Cariboo, Atlin, Wild Horse and Cassiar were in the fore and thousands of argonauts endured hardships, loneliness and occasionally misfortune in their quest for bonanza creeks. They covered the entire province; from Atlin to the Boundary Country, from the East Kootenay to Vancouver Island - no creek was too small to prospect, no region too remote to explore. A renowned few succeeded and names like "Cariboo" Cameron, Billy Barker, Fritz Miller, Robert Stevenson, Bill Cunningham and Adam Beam endure to this day. But they were only a minute part of the whole, because the majority of these men died in obscurity, often virtually penniless, chasing their own rainbows to the last. They were a special breed, individuals who had been drawn by the wilderness and never left it - living by their own creeds and following a precarious existence for their entire lives. Even today, in the back country of the province, there are a number of prospectors who have chosen this way of life, extracting their tithe from the gold creeks each season, content with their lot.

The information in this work is not intended for the experienced placer miner but rather for laymen and novices who are interested in the fundamentals of placer mining and the techniques of panning, that simplest of all mining methods. The notes also cover the histories of many of the major placer gold creeks of British Columbia. Some other knowledge basic to the beginning panner or other individuals who find themselves engrossed with this most rewarding pursuit, is included as well.

BACKGROUND

Of all the metals known to man none has captured his imagination more than gold has. It is the most celebrated of the "noble" metals, renowned for its many properties, of which rarity, beauty, malleability, high lustre and value are but a few.

The earliest written records contain innumerable references to gold, often describing in great detail its many uses. In fact nearly all of the advanced early civilizations prized it to a high degree, with their most valued possessions invariably fashioned from the metal.

Archaeological finds in Egypt, Greece, Rome, Asia Minor and almost every other part of the old Mediterranean world indicate that the many peoples of that region and era were well versed and familiar with the uses of the metal. In south and central America, the ancient Incans, Mayans, Aztecs and others also utilized gold to a high degree.

For centuries men have been engaged in the search for gold, often devoting their entire lives in their attempts to locate the precious metal; some in the pursuit of actual or legendary treasures or lost mines; such as the renowned Oak Island Treasure and The Lost Dutchman Mine, others in the actual mining of the metal in either lode or placer deposits.

The physical characteristics of gold are also impressive. It is an unusually durable metal, impervious to nearly all natural or artificial elements – with the exception of a few acids. It is interesting to note that doubloons, Louis d'or, eagles and other gold coins and objects have been recovered from sunken wrecks at great depths and usually emerge as brilliant as the day they were lost. It requires an amazing temperature, in excess of 1900 degrees Fahrenheit before it melts. Other properties are also noteworthy, its specific gravity is 19.25 which means that it is 19¼ times as heavy as an equal volume of water and a cube of pure gold measuring 6" each way would weigh slightly more than 180 pounds. Quite a remarkable metal in many respects.

Over the centuries it has been the subject of speculation, myth and exaggeration. In the Americas, the Spanish conquistadores, inspired by stories of "El Dorado" and "The Seven Cities of Cibola," explored both trackless wastes and unmapped jungles in their persistent attempts to find these fabled places. And the search has continued right into modern times. The rushes to California then to the Cariboo and the Yukon in the nineteenth century electrified the continent and much of the fascination surrounding this precious metal emanated from those colourful eras. And it has continued to attract individuals in all walks of life and will probably continue to do so as long as men are intrigued by gold, the king of metals.

A BRIEF HISTORY

Since 1858 the recorded placer gold production in British Columbia has amounted to nearly $100,000,000. Of this total almost half was yielded by the creeks and rivers of the famous Cariboo, and the remainder from various other gold producing regions in the province, ranging from the

Atlin field in the extreme north-western corner to the Boundary region, which almost straddles the International Boundary, to the south.

The first reports of placer gold in British Columbia pre-date 1858. Although there are several conflicting accounts gold may have been found in the Kamloops area as early as 1852. By 1855, American placer miners had found gold on the Pend d'Oreille, a river which joins the Columbia near Trail in the West Kootenay area.

Surprisingly, although the gold placers of California were on the wane at the time, little interest was shown in the new discoveries in British Columbia. By 1857, however, when placers near the mouth of the Nicomen began yielding exciting quantities of gold. Rumours of the find quickly filtered south to San Francisco. The electrifying news touched off a hectic stampede and by the spring of 1858 the first contingent of argonauts from California reached Fort Victoria. By that summer the exodus from the Golden State turned into a flood as almost 25,000 miners arrived in the province. On their way up "Fraser's river," they tested the bars as they went and found magnificent diggings on bars like Hills, Boston, China and scores more.

By 1859 a vanguard of prospectors had pushed northward, exploring the tributaries as they went. At the forks of the Quesnel they discovered good pay and there they paused, unaware that they were on the threshold of the prolific Cariboo goldfields. In 1860 rich ground was discovered on Antler Creek, and in the south, in the Boundary Country, Rock Creek had proven to be bonanza diggings.

The following year great strikes were made on Williams, Lightning, Lowhee, Slough and other gold-bearing streams in the heart of Cariboo. It was the beginning of the golden era.

By 1863 another amazing find was made when coarse gold was found in Wild Horse Creek in the East Kootenay and by 1864 there was activity in the Big Bend Region as French and McCulloch creeks drew attention.

By 1869 the Omineca began to come into its own when creeks like Vital and Manson became important producers. Four years later, as the miners penetrated even farther north, the Cassiar District came to prominence as Thibert, Dease and McDame creeks all proved bonanza diggings.

Attention shifted in 1885 to the Similkameen when Granite Creek, a tributary of the Tulameen river, and ignored for almost a quarter of a century, was discovered to be rich in both gold and platinum.

In 1898, the second richest placer gold district in the history of British Columbia came to the fore when Miller and McLaren hammered the first stakes into ground overlooking Pine Creek. For most of the latter part of the century the Atlin District attracted the attention, and also yielded more placer gold, than any other region in the province.

But Atlin was the last of the historic stampedes and although a few intermittent and occasionally exciting finds, like Cedar Creek in 1921, were made thereafter, the great heyday of placer mining was over.

Today, with the price of gold well over $200 an ounce, there are an increasing number of people taking up where the prospectors of yesterday left off, prospecting along historic creeks of the past in quest of the royal metal known as gold.

(7)

I
THE
GOLD PAN

Panning is the simplest and the most inexpensive of all the methods used to recover placer gold. Although the origin of the gold pan, the device used in panning, is obscure, some authorities believe that it came into use among the miners of Transylvania, in the central part of Europe, no later than the 15th century and possibly before then. In the alluvial goldfields of North America, Australia, South Africa and in most other parts of the world except South and Central America, it was, and is, the prospectors' inseparable companion, ideally suited to test any gravels which are indicative of carrying placer gold.

The gold pan is generally made of sheet iron, although a few are rarely made of copper. It is shaped like a dish with flaring straight sides and is flat on the bottom. The pan may vary from 10" to 18" in diameter at the top and from 2" to 4" in depth. The pan which is used by most placer men is approximately 15" in diameter at the top and is 3" deep and has a rounded lip. This type of pan is the "Australian" pan. The "American" pan is similar, the basic difference is the lip, which is straight on the "American" pan.

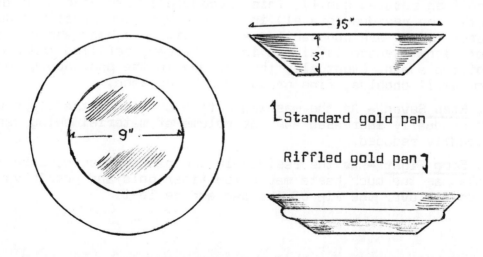

15"

3"

9"

Standard gold pan

Riffled gold pan

The technique for panning gold, which varies considerably from miner to miner, should, if possible, be learned from an experienced placer man but as this may not be feasible certain steps have been outlined in this chapter to facilitate the beginning panner. Anyone, regardless of age or experience, can with practise, become an expert panner.

The Various Steps in Gold Panning are Listed Below:

LEARNING TO PAN

1. Step One - If your gold pan is new and is metal make sure that the greasy protective film is removed before you start panning. To remove this layer heat the pan over a campfire or a stove for a few minutes. When the pan is removed from the fire remember that the pan retains heat for some time and should be handled gingerly at first.

2. Step Two - When arriving at a panning spot the gold pan should be filled with gravel (preferably bedrock gravel). The amount of 'dirt' in the pan varies from individual to individual but try not to over-load your pan.

3. Step Three - The pan is then submerged in the stream; if possible in fairly slow moving water (swift water tends to carry off the fine gold particles) and then rotated rapidly from side to side. This is done so that the water penetrates the gravel and the gold, which is heavier, will work its way toward the bottom of the pan.

4. Step Four - The gravel in the gold pan is then worked thoroughly by hand-mixing the 'dirt' with the water in the pan. All clay lumps should be broken up and the larger pebbles and rocks removed from the pan by drawing the fingers 'loosely' across the gravel and scooping out the rocks. The next step is actually panning the contents.

5. Step Five - The gold pan is held (at first) in an almost horizontal position but tilted slightly downward and away from the body so that the water in the pan can wash the lighter material out over the lip of the pan. The gravel in the pan should be kept near the lip of the pan at all times so that excess gravel can escape with the water as it is tilted out of the pan.

6. Step Six - The pan is then dipped in the creek, filled with water and then rotated gently. This procedure is repeated time after time until the residue (gravel) in the pan has been greatly reduced. The larger rocks are constantly removed with one hand and after several rotations the pan is dipped in the stream, refilled with water, and rotated again. Eventually the residue in the pan should consist of a few small pebbles, fine gravel and black sand.

7. Step Seven - As the washing action continues the slope of the pan is gradually increased and the volume of material being panned out is steadily reduced.

8. Step Eight - As the residue in the pan decreases, care should be taken as too much haste may allow finer gold and possibly a nugget to wash out over the lip of the pan and be lost.

9. <u>Step Nine</u> - Eventually the material remaining in the gold pan should consist almost entirely of black sand and the finer particles of gold known as "colours." By 'tailing' the pan the gold may be observed. At this point it would be wise to stop panning and pick out the visible gold with tweezers, or if it's coarse enough, by hand.

10. <u>Step Ten</u> - The remaining black sand should be saved. In order to keep this residue (which usually carries some fine particles of gold) it should be placed in a canvas bag or container to be separated at a more convenient time later.

11. <u>Step Eleven</u> - The black sand should be thoroughly dried. This may be accomplished by placing the black sand in a pan and setting the pan over a campfire. When the black sand is heated (and dry), it should be dumped onto a piece of fairly stiff paper. A good magnet may then be placed under the paper and drawn along. The black sand will be drawn off, leaving only gold and dirt behind. If a magnet is not available the gold may be separated from the black sand by placing the black sand in a gold pan and gently "blowing" the black sand. The black sand will blow away from the heavier gold if this operation is done carefully. It is a skill which requires both skill and patience but can be easily mastered after several attempts. In the Similkameen-Tulameen area of the province it should be remembered that using a magnet to separate the gold and platinum from the black sand is hazardous because almost half of the platinum from that **area is magnetic** and a magnet attracts the platinum with the black sand.

12. <u>Step Twelve</u> - The recovered gold should be weighed and stored in a container and placed in safekeeping.

<u>Note</u> - There are several important points to remember when panning. Water should be used in abundance because when water is mixed with the gravel in the pan it causes the gold to work to the bottom of the pan where it should be. Gold is seldom lost by using too much water but is often lost by failing to use enough. It is also important to remember that while panning, the gravel in the pan should always be kept near the lip of the pan so that excess and lighter material can "wash out" when the water is washed out. Under ideal conditions a panner can pan out more than one hundred pans of paydirt per miners (ten hour) day.

<u>How to Recognize Gold</u> - Gold is easily recognizeable from particles of mica, which is sometimes referred to as "fool's gold," because mica is light in weight and brittle, whereas gold is heavy and also malleable. Most placer gold is similar in colour to a common gold ring although in some regions it takes on a coppery, brassy or even greenish hue due to the presence in the metal of other minerals. Occasionally placer gold will be heavily oxidized (stained). If placer platinum is present in the pan (as it may be in the Similkameen-Tulameen region), it is recognized by its silver colour and its heavy weight. It should not generally be mistaken for lead as the latter is dull grey in colour.

II

BEDROCK

"Bedrock" is one of the most important words in placer mining. It is on this impervious layer where well over 90% of all the placer gold in British Columbia has been recovered. There are a number of points concerning "bedrock" with which every placer miner should be familiar. Some of them are:

1. The Definition of Bedrock - Usually a continuous layer of rock upon which placer gold settles because of water action. Sometimes this layer is heavily fractured, cracked or broken and when it is the gold tends to collect in the cracks and crevices, especially, but not always under large rocks on the bedrock.

2. The Location of Bedrock - In mountainous country and near creeks and rivers with a steep gradient (slope), bedrock is usually close at hand. In valleys like the Fraser Valley and other river valleys where the river is generally slow moving, bedrock is usually far below the surface of the river or at the extreme perimeter of the valley. In their early stages most streams and rivers cut through bedrock as they flow down from the higher levels. Hopefully, bedrock on a gold bearing stream or river will be found on or close to the surface. Bedrock deeper than eight feet under the surface gravels is generally not economically feasible to work unless the values are exceptionally high because mechanized equipment would have to be used in order to mine it.

3. Types of Bedrock - There are, of course, all kinds of bedrock. In some districts there are half a dozen distinct types of bedrock which yield placer gold. In the Cariboo black, reddish, yellowish, grey and varying other shades in between are known to carry gold. Experienced miners everywhere are always on the lookout for bedrock which is coloured. Red oxidized bedrock has yielded extremely well in areas like the Boundary, Cariboo, Kootenay, Similkameen, Cassiar and several other regions. Smooth bedrock often does not hold gold. Old hands look for bedrock which is heavily creviced, cracked, fractured or rough.

4. <u>Clay on Bedrock</u> - When clay is tight on bedrock, that is covering bedrock, gold is almost never found on the bedrock. Old placer
men seldom check bedrock which is tight against clay. Walk by it.

5. <u>High Bedrock</u> - Bedrock may be found far above the present levels
of creeks or rivers. Bedrock located on high benches often carries
placer gold. Obviously, in times past, the streams ran in channels
which were higher than today. Erosion cut the channels deeper but
the gold stayed behind. The Similkameen-Tulameen, East Kootenay,
Cariboo, Boundary and many other historic old mining districts had
high ancient channels which were often hundreds of feet above the
present channels but yielded exceptionally rich placers. Always be
on the look-out for high bedrock which could carry gold.

6. <u>Worked Bedrock</u> - In numerous instances in the past century or
so, bedrock which has already been "cleaned" at one time has later
yielded good returns. In the majority of the creeks worked by the
Chinese miners of the past it is generally logical to assume that
the bedrock they cleaned is not worth bothering about because they
were usually thorough and missed very little gold. In other areas,
however, specifically where an initial stampede took place in the
1860s, the first miners on the ground were often anxious to mine
out their ground rapidly so that they could move on to other and
perhaps richer ground, that in some instances they cleaned their
bedrock carelessly. In most cases they simply did not break down
the bedrock as deeply as they should have thus missing cracks and
crevices which later proved to carry considerable quantities of
gold. Sometimes they did not bother to mine under an exceptionally
large boulder which was lying on bedrock. Check to see if it has
been "propped" or "undercut," if it hasn't (unlikely) it should be
moved with a "come-along" and the bedrock under where it originally stood should be carefully cleaned.

7. <u>False Bedrock</u> - This is a phrase applied to "hardpan," a hard
layer of clay which looks like true bedrock and if often mistaken
for it. As this layer occasionally holds gold inexperienced miners
sometimes neglect to penetrate through it to true bedrock. There
are a number of famous instances in the annals of British Columbia
mining history where a "false" bedrock was penetrated to the true
bedrock and amazing amounts of placer gold was recovered.

<u>Note</u> - <u>Some Errors Made When Cleaning Bedrock</u> - There are several
common mistakes made when inexperienced or careless miners "clean"
bedrock. The most common error is the failure to penetrate bedrock
deep enough (especially when the bedrock is heavily fractured), a
surprising amount of gold can often be recovered from cracks which
have penetrated deeply into the bedrock. Another mistake which is
usual is neglecting to scrape off (or wash) muddy rocks and slabs
when breaking bedrock. Quite often the mud on these pieces of rock
will carry significant quantities of gold.

III
SNIPING

The word "sniping" is used to describe the practice of working or re-working bedrock in order to recover gold. Sniping is one of the most fascinating occupations in placer mining and good snipers will often recover astonishing amounts of gold (which is usually coarse and nuggety). Some prospectors become so adept at sniping that they never mine any other way, preferring to snipe and take the chance of good returns or none at all.

Williams Creek, Cariboo, from a painting by Whymper - circa 1864.

1. <u>Sniping on Bedrock</u> - Naturally the best returns by the sniper are from bedrock. There are snipers who work the same crevices and cracks on favourite creeks or rivers every season during low water (the best time for sniping), and recover gold every year. This is a fascinating method of placer mining as some crevices and cracks will surrender a considerable amount of gold, especially if they have never been worked by a sniper before.

2. <u>Sniping Around Boulders</u> - Experienced snipers concentrate on large rocks and boulders (especially when they lie directly on or just over bedrock). They mine under and around these boulders during the low water in the spring and fall each season, aware that these obstacles act like river riffles and tend to stop and trap the gold coming down the river. It is not unusual to obtain several ounces of gold which is extremely coarse and nuggety from under a boulder. Experienced and observant placer men examine all large boulders (the larger boulders trap more gold than smaller ones) to determine whether they have been moved by previous generations of miners. In most instances they have and sometimes there is evidence that this is the case, especially if there are smaller rocks or timbers propped under the larger boulder. The Chinese were experts at propping and then mining under the rock to get the gold. Occasionally a large boulder can be levered out of position by using pry bars but more often a come-along or power-pull with a sling and a cable are required. Be cautious when working near boulders as they sometimes shift or fall unexpectedly. There are many instances recorded where even experienced placer miners were killed when undercutting a boulder - play it safe.

3. <u>Sniping Crevices and Cracks</u> - All efficient and successful snipers carry several pieces of equipment necessary for cleaning out cracks and crevices in bedrock. A large pry bar is necessary for breaking, prying and levering pieces of bedrock or for widening a crevice so that it can be cleaned with a smaller crevicing tool. A smaller tool (sometimes a long screwdriver or a narrow 6" pick) is invaluable in cleaning out narrow cracks. A small whisk broom is also handy when a crack or crevice has to be cleaned. A pair of tweezers is a must.

<u>Note</u> - Unless sniping "high" bedrock which is far above the creek or river, this operation should be conducted only during the low water periods in the early spring and the fall. During high water the best paying (lowest) sections of bedrock are covered with water and cannot be effectively sniped, so wait until the water is at its lowest level in the spring or fall. Another tip is to be on the lookout for a rock generally called "ironstone." Ironstone is usually small, invariably rounded, blackish in colour (sometimes with a reddish sheen) and is very heavy. Being so heavy it tends to go where the gold travels and is known as an 'indicator' rock. Where you find ironstone the gold is not far away.

IV

How to Build a
SLUICEBOX

Miners watching the sluice-flumes and sluice-boxes on Spruce Creek in the Atlin District in 1905.   (Provincial Archives)

Sluicing is the most efficient method of recovering placer gold in a mining operation after it has been determined by testing that the ground merits mining. Some larger placer mining operations that process hundreds of cubic yards of dirt each day usually use a series of sluice-boxes which may extend for more than a hundred feet with a width of four or five feet. Long sluice-boxes are required only when a great volume of water is required to efficiently process the pay-dirt or where a considerable amount of clay is present in the gravel. In a one or two man operation, however, especially where the gold is coarse and nuggety, a 12 foot sluice-box will suffice and sometimes a 6 or 8 foot box can do the job.

When clay is present in the gravels a longer sluice-box should be used because clay requires more time and water to break it up. The gradient (slope) of the sluice, therefore, should be increased and the length of the sluice also increased.

The following particulars should be considered when constructing a small sluice-box.

1. Construction - Most small sluice-boxes are made of wood although sometimes aluminum or another metal is used in construction but the cost is generally higher when metals are used. Experienced hands make their sluice-boxes from reasonably dry yellow pine. Always check the material to see that it's free from knots and pitch and to make sure that it isn't warped. Generally woods like spruce, cedar and even fir are avoided because they aren't hardy enough to withstand the continual wear and tear on a sluice-box. The material should be sanded, especially on the bottom of the box where the riffles are placed. The diagrams below can be referred to when constructing an 8' sluice.

Step One - Obtain the necessary material for the basic sluice-box. One eight foot x 12" x 1" yellow pine board and two eight foot x 8" x 1" boards. Check to make sure that the material is free from all knots, cracks, pitch and isn't warped.

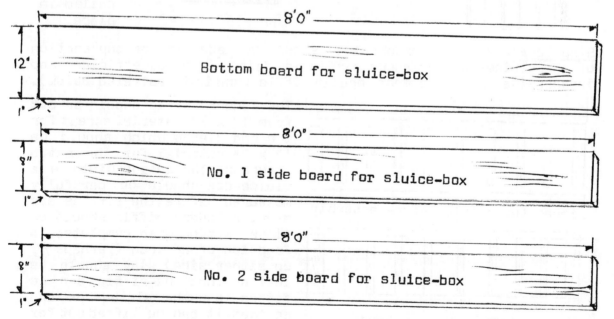

8'0"
12"
1"
Bottom board for sluice-box

8'0"
8"
1"
No. 1 side board for sluice-box

8'0"
8"
1"
No. 2 side board for sluice-box

Step Two - Fit the side boards on the bottom board and nail with care. Observe the method of nailing the sides onto the bottom board. Follow the diagram below to make sure the side boards are placed correctly.

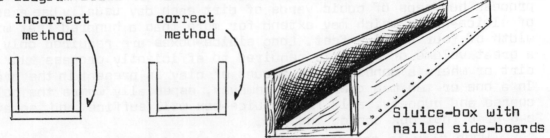

incorrect method   correct method

Sluice-box with nailed side-boards

Note: If the side boards are nailed to the bottom incorrectly, fine gold and flat nuggets may be lost in the horizontal cracks on both sides.

When the side boards are nailed in the correct way the vertical cracks in the sides cannot rob the sluice-box of gold.

Step Three - The side boards on the sluice-box have to be braced so that the sluice will be stronger. It is also easier to carry a sluice-box with good braces on it. Generally three braces are used in an 8' box. The material used for bracing is usually 1" thick, 3" wide and long enough so that they extend the width of the sluice-box.

Cut three braces (3" x 1" x 14").
Drill holes for the nails before nailing to the sluice otherwise the wood on the brace might split and weaken it.

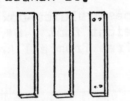

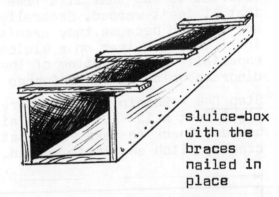

sluice-box with the braces nailed in place

Step Four - A riffle of about 4' should be made for the top section of the sluice-box. A ladder riffle is fairly simple, efficient and inexpensive. It is the most popular riffle (and is illustrated below).

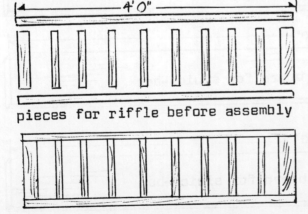

4' 0"

pieces for riffle before assembly

ladder riffle after assembly

The ladder riffle should be cut from 1" x 1" material except for the end pieces which should be 1" x 2" material for the extra strength. The inside width of a sluice-box should be carefully measured before the riffles are made. A ladder riffle should be close fitting when completed. A fraction of an inch (perhaps $\frac{1}{16}$" on either side) play should be left so that the riffle can be fitted into the sluice-box and so that it can be lifted out for clean-ups without binding.

A view of the sluice-box as it looks with a 4' 0" ladder riffle in place. The riffle should slide into the box relatively easily. Burlap, indoor-outdoor carpeting or some other rough material can also be placed under the riffles to hold fine gold. The riffle can be kept in place by toe-nailing the riffles to the sides of the sluice-box. When "cleaning-up," the nails used to hold the riffle in place may be removed. When the clean-up is finished the riffle is put back in the sluice-box and the nails hammered back in place.

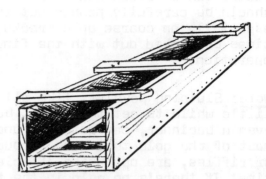

4. The sluice-box with a ladder riffle in place

Step Five - After the ladder riffle has been constructed and fitted into the sluice-box, an expanded metal mesh riffle should be placed in the lower part of the box. Expanded metal mesh can be purchased in some hardware stores or from a tinsmith. The expanded metal riffle should be cut so that it slides easily into the sluice-box. The usual practice is to place burlap, indoor-outdoor carpeting or another type of rough cloth under the expanded metal mesh so that the fine placer gold will stick to it.

Step Six - The sluice-box should be ready for use now. Choose a gold creek and set the box near the stream. Make sure the box has a fair gradient (slope), so that the water, when turned in, will run through relatively rapidly. When the sluice-box is set and the water is running through evenly, start shoveling dirt into the box. Always make sure that the top of the ladder riffles are visible because if they aren't gold may run right through the box. Check the box and pan the tailings (the dirt running through the box) to see if any placer gold is escaping. If any gold is running through the box the gradient is probably too steep. Make adjustments and continue sluicing.

Step Seven - After shoveling into the box for some time (usually half a day or a full day), the box is "cleaned-up." The clean-up operation is important and several points should be remembered. The water flow through the sluice-box should be cut down until only a partial flow is going through the box. Next the box is "washed down," that is, in mining. parlance, washing most of the dirt through the box until only the concentrates (black sand, ironstone, gold) remain in the riffles. A large gold pan or pail should be placed at the end of the down end of the box before the riffles are lifted. The miner should then lift the ladder (first) riffle and pick out all visible gold. After this operation has been completed the second (metal mesh) riffle should be lifted. After both of the riffles have been removed the burlap should be removed and carefully rolled and put in a pail (to be rinsed at a more convenient time to obtain the fine gold adhering to it) The box, with a trickle of water still going through it, should be "whisked" with a broom or whisk to make sure all of the gold left in the box is swept into the pail under the end of the sluice. Finally, after the sluice-box is clean and checked, the "concentrates" in the container should be carefully panned out to recover the gold. In some regions, especially on coarse gold creeks, nuggets and coarser gold can sometimes be picked out with the fingers or tweezers during the clean-up operation.

Note: Sluicing paydirt, like all operations is placer mining takes a little while to get the knack, but after several days almost anyone, even a beginner, can get the fundamentals down so that he is saving most of the gold that goes through the box. To make sure that a box, or riffles, are operating efficiently check the tailings from time to time. If there's no gold in the tailings (the material that has been washed through the sluice-box) the box is probably operating fairly well.

Some placer miners on famous Spruce Creek in the Atlin District in 1905. This is a typical mining operation of the day. In the centre of the photograph is a lengthy sluice-box which three of the miners are shoveling into. The man nearest the sluice-box watches the gravel in the box, removing blocked rocks and watching the riffles. Spruce was one of the premier placer creeks in the province and produced almost 10 tons of gold during its heyday, ranking it behind Williams Creek and Lightning Creek, both in the Cariboo District.

THE ROCKER

Miners using rockers on Gold Hill in the Yukon in 1898.

A rocker, also called a "cradle" or a "dolly," is used when water is in short supply or when the gradient of a river or stream is too shallow to permit the use of a sluice-box, which is far more efficient. Rockers, probably invented in either the Carolinas or Georgia in the early 1800s, was used extensively in the West.

This simple device, constructed mainly of wood and usually referred to as a rocker, is relatively inexpensive to build and ennables a miner to wash perhaps 3 cubic yards of gold-bearing gravel per day.

The rocker is generally constructed of either 1" or ¾" lumber, a piece of metal screen, metal or wooden riffles and a blanket or burlap. The sizes vary considerably but generally a relatively small size is the most common because of its easiness to move. The one disadvantage of the smaller rockers, however, is that they are not as efficient in recovering finer gold as larger rockers. The larger rockers, however, usually require two men to operate efficiently and are considerably more difficult to transport from place to place unless they are held together by nuts and bolts instead of the conventional nails - the former construction ennables them to be "knocked down" when they require moving.

Rockers can only be used in specific areas and are usually set up either close by a bank of a creek or river where water is readily available. The water can be either piped or bailed into the tray. It is important that the flow of water into the tray be relatively steady or consistent as any fluctuations tend to wash the fine gold through the sluice.

Occasionally the gold-bearing gravel will be mixed with clay, this situation makes the operation considerably more difficult. Sometimes the problem is solved by "puddling" the material in a separate box before it is placed in the rocker. If the gold is mixed throughout the clay the box where the puddling has taken place would require separate panning.

Generally the operation of a rocker is more reliable when two miners are working, one shovelling the gravel in and then dumping the tray when the gravel is washed, and the other rocking and bailing water. The man who is required to dump the tray should be careful in regions where coarse gold and nuggets are commonplace as it is possible to throw out a nugget with the gravel remaining in the tray if the residue is not carefully examined. It must be realized that the larger nuggets will be too large to pass through the ½" punched holes in the tray.

When the tray is filled water is then poured over the gravel at the same time that the box is being rocked back and forth. This action causes the gold to head for the apron or riffles and remain there. The movement of the rocker should be fairly easy as violent motions tend to wash gold as well as gravel over the riffles. Ordinarily, however, fine gold passes through the punched holes and is caught on either the apron or riffles. It is a wise practice to pan the tailings or waste from time to time to determine whether gold is being lost during the operation. If the gravel being worked is rich both apron and sluice riffles should be cleaned up frequently, otherwise gold could escape over clogged apron or riffles. The apron must also be taken out when it is seen that it requires washing. The accumulated residue, usually both gold and black sand, may be washed into a bucket and panned later as time permits. When the sluice riffles need cleaning a pan should be placed across the mouth of the box and the residue washed into it. Again, the contents are carefully panned. If any canvas or burlap is used under the riffles this should also be washed.

It should be remembered that the rocker is an essentially simple and inexpensive device used to recover gold in areas which are too large for panning and not large enough for more costly methods of mining. It should also be borne in mind that once one becomes used to operating a rocker that it will generally wash approximately four times the volume of gravel that an experienced hand can wash with a gold pan.

The Detailed Plans for Building a Rocker

The first part of this chapter discusses the operation and some of the uses of a rocker as well as a sketch of a rocker and some simple plans. It is conceivable, however, that some of our readers may want a more detailed plan of a rocker and the exact directions on how to go about building one. Although there are various sizes of rockers and a few slight variations in types, the one on which the plans and directions are given on the next two pages is a standard type. The officers of the Department of Mines of the province of British Columbia drew up both the plans and the directions in Bulletin No. 21, issued by the Department in 1959. The average individual should, without too much difficulty, be able to build a reliable rocker from the diagrams and directions given.

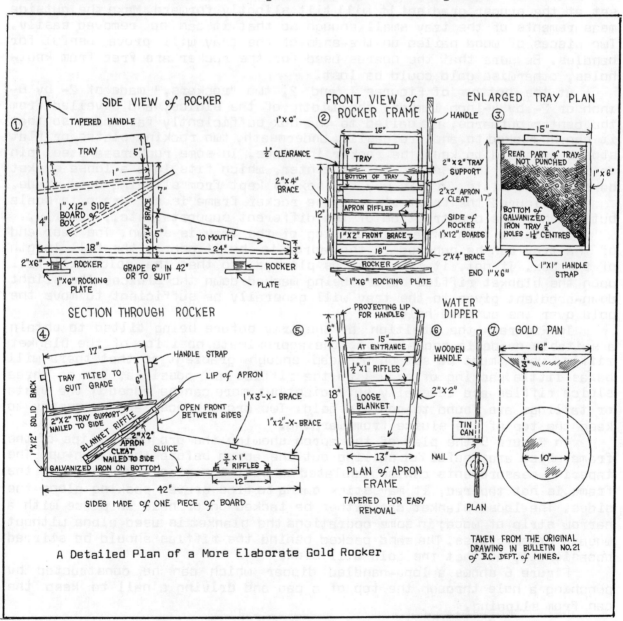

A Detailed Plan of a More Elaborate Gold Rocker

Building a rocker

(Department of Mines Bulletin No. 21 "Notes on Placer Mining in B.C.)

Figure 1 is the side view of a rocker showing the 2- by 4-inch side braces nailed to the side-boards of the box. One of these is extended and tapered for a handle. Each side of the box and sluice can be cut out of one piece of 1- by 12-inch lumber, 42 inches or more in length. The bottom of the box, shown in Figure 2, can be made of one piece of board 16 inches wide and 42 inches long. If not procurable, two pieces planed so that they fit tightly together can be used. It is safer to cover the bottom of the sluice with canvas, galvanized iron, or tin to prevent leakage, and, in the latter case, assist the flow of sand and gravel. The tray, which is built of 1- by 6-inch lumber, 17 inches long, with screening or a punched galvanized plate nailed to the bottom or held in place with a 1- by ½-inch wooden strap, is set upon two 2- by 2-inch supports nailed to the side of the box at an angle sufficiently great so that when the entire rocker is set at the proper gradient it will tilt slightly forward. Make the outside measurements of the tray small enough so that it can be removed easily. Two pieces of wood nailed on the ends of the tray will prove useful for handles. Be sure that the boards used for the rocker are free from knot-holes, otherwise gold could be lost.

At the bottom of Figures 1 and 2, two "rockers," made of 2- by 6-inch or 2- by 4-inch lumber, the width of the sluice, and bevelled from the center outwards, are nailed to the box sufficiently far apart so that it can be rocked to and fro easily. Underneath, two rocking plates or flat stones are laid to keep the rocker in place. In some rockers a steel pin or large spike is inserted in the center, which fits into a loose socket bored in the plate. In this way the box is kept from slipping down-grade.

In Figure 2 the front view of the rocker frame is not drawn to scale but to show the construction of the different supports, etc., clearly.

In Figure 3 an enlarged drawing of the tray is shown. The rear end of the tray can be punched if the apron is built nearly the full length of the box. If not, it is better as planned, so that the gold will fall upon the blanket riffles before being washed down the sluice. The slight down-gradient given to the tray will generally be sufficient to move the gold over the punched holes.

In Figure 4 the position of the tray before being tilted to obtain a suitable grade is shown. Also, the approximate position of the blanket riffle, which must be set on a steep enough gradient so that there will be as little packing of gravel on the riffles as possible. Two or three sluice riffles are generally sufficient but more can be added if the waste or tailings are found to contain gold. Two cross-braces are necessary to keep the top of the sluice from warping.

In Figure 5 the plan of the apron showing the projecting lips of the frame which are useful for pulling out the apron before the clean-up. The tapering measurements can be regulated to suit the size of the box. If the frame is not tapered, it may stick owing to fine gravel packing along the sides. The loose blanket can either be tacked on or held in place with a narrow strip of wood; in some operations the blanket is used alone without wooden cross-pieces. The sand packed behind the riffles should be stirred occasionally so that the gold will sink.

Figure 6 shows a long-handled dipper which can be constructed by punching a hole through the top of a can and driving a nail to keep the can from slipping.

VI
ATLIN

INTRODUCTION

Atlin — The region surrounding the historic town of Atlin was the scene of the last great placer gold rush in British Columbia and marked the end of a colourful and never-to-be-forgotten era which had begun on the distant Fraser River only forty years before.

The initial discovery of gold in the area was credited to one George F. Miller, a close-mouthed hotel owner out of Juneau, Alaska. In 1896, acting on directions and following a map purportedly given him by a dying prospector whom he had befriended, Miller made his way deep into Canadian territory and on an unnamed creek flowing from the east into remote Atlin Lake he paused and tested the gravels — and within minutes he realized that he had struck it rich. Soon after short supplies forced him to return to Juneau, but with the Klondike excitement at its height, Miller bided his time, confiding his amazing discovery to only a few close and trusted friends. Finally, in 1898, he disclosed the exact location to his younger brother Fritz and a Canadian from Nova Scotia named Kenneth McLaren. In the spring of that year these two located and staked the stream which became known as Pine Creek, a creek which was eventually to prove immensely rich.

Big Jack's Claim on Boulder Creek in the Atlin district in 1903. Standing to the right of the sluicebox is Big Jack. Boulder Creek was one of the premier creeks in the area. (Archives photograph)

So Fritz Miller and Kenneth McLaren became known as "The Founders of Atlin Camp," although it is highly debatable whether either of these two or even George Miller actually deserve that distinction. It is conceivable that the real credit may belong to a more shadowy figure, the old miner who reputedly gave the location of the gold creek to the elder Miller. Although the details are hazy after three-quarters of a century there is some historical evidence to substantiate this theory. It is fairly evident that George Miller must have had exact directions which he was able to follow to locate the previously unknown creek in almost trackless wilds, and two years later was able to give explicit directions to his younger brother Fritz, which in turn ennabled the latter to find the gold creek. Unfortunately, Fritz Miller's diaries, which probably could have provided the missing details, disappeared after his untimely death in 1901. Several reliable sources, including the highly respected volumes written by Howay and Scholefield, state that the first arrivals on Pine Creek found old workings which indicated that other prospectors had been there far before 1898:

> "Then came the (Atlin) stampede of 1898. The new-comers found old and rotten sluice boxes and other evidence that the former generation of miners had penetrated this vicinity many years before."

Thus, the "dying miner" theory, although highly romantic, may indeed have been accurate and the old prospector supposedly befriended by George Miller may have been the last member of the mysterious band of miners

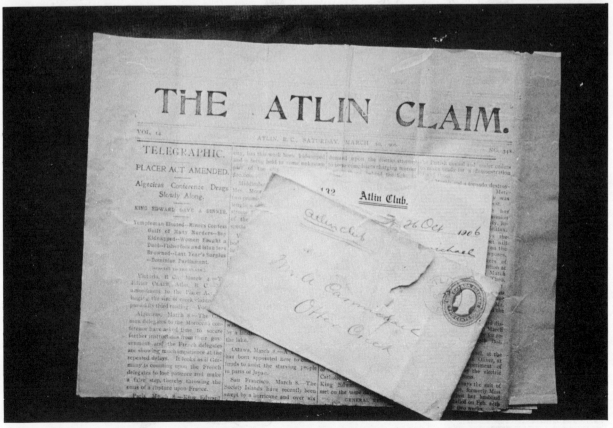

A copy of the famous ATLIN CLAIM, March 10, 1906.

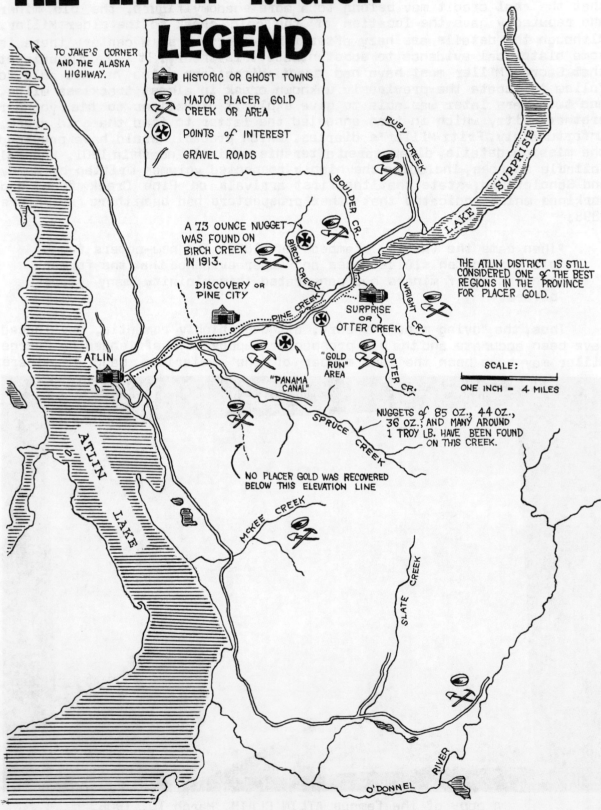

THE ATLIN REGION

LEGEND

- HISTORIC OR GHOST TOWNS
- MAJOR PLACER GOLD CREEK OR AREA
- POINTS of INTEREST
- GRAVEL ROADS

TO JAKE'S CORNER AND THE ALASKA HIGHWAY.

A 73 OUNCE NUGGET WAS FOUND ON BIRCH CREEK IN 1913.

DISCOVERY or PINE CITY

THE ATLIN DISTRICT IS STILL CONSIDERED ONE of THE BEST REGIONS IN THE PROVINCE FOR PLACER GOLD.

RUBY CREEK

LAKE SURPRISE

BOULDER CR.

BIRCH CREEK

PINE CREEK

SURPRISE OR OTTER CREEK

WRIGHT CR.

"GOLD RUN" AREA

OTTER CR.

"PANAMA CANAL"

ATLIN

ATLIN LAKE

SCALE: ONE INCH = 4 MILES

SPRUCE CREEK

NUGGETS of 85 OZ., 44 OZ., 36 OZ.; AND MANY AROUND 1 TROY LB. HAVE BEEN FOUND ON THIS CREEK.

NO PLACER GOLD WAS RECOVERED BELOW THIS ELEVATION LINE

MCKEE CREEK

SLATE CREEK

O'DONNEL RIVER

who mined on Pine Creek prior to the 1898 rush. However, who these first prospectors were, where they came from, why they disappeared and where they went, remains an unsolved mystery to this day.

And Pine Creek was only the first of a maze of placer gold streams in the region which were to provide a golden harvest to Atlin miners for years. Others, like McKee, Ruby, Boulder, Birch and Wright all added their share of the metal and one of them, Spruce, even surpassed its illustrious sister Pine Creek, in total production.

So, over the years, the creeks from this almost unknown corner of the province have produced almost half a million fine ounces of gold, worth, at today's prices, more than $150 million and continue to produce in very interesting quantities to this day.

Although far off the beaten path and invariably bypassed by the unknowing, the Atlin area is perhaps the most memorable and one of the most scenic regions in the province. Atlin itself has kept some of its links with the past and the surrounding area is, in many ways, still reminiscent of the placer years: the gaunt ghost of Discovery overlooks Pine Creek today as it did three-quarters of a century ago when that ghost town was a city and the argonauts worked the rich gravels below. There are other reminders along the placer streams too; derelict waterwheels, abandoned shafts, deserted cabins and obsolete equipment.

Atlin is indeed a remembered place.

The Atlin Mining Company's hydraulic operations on McKee Creek in August of 1903. On the extreme right is Richard McBride who in June of that year had become premier of British Columbia. (Provincial Archives photograph)

THE PLACER CREEKS

Birch Creek - Discovered in 1898, this creek parallels Boulder and Ruby although it is west of Lake Surprise and flows into Pine creek, instead of the lake. In the boom years it was largely ignored as the depth of bed-rock discouraged hand-mining operations. Later, when the easy-to-work diggings in other creeks were nearing exhaustion, attention again turned to Birch.

The greatest period of activity took place between 1902 and the start of the First World War although there was considerable activity during the thirties and even today.

Some of the best results were obtained by large outfits like the huge Dominion Trust Company who hydraulicked extensively and took out appreciable amounts of gold prior to 1913. Other operations, both large and small, have obtained occasionally excellent results.

Deep overburden and the often indefinite location of the ancient channel sometimes made mining operations unprofitable on this stream although it too, like other Atlin creeks, had miners who worked it for years in preference to any other.

It is worthy of mention that the largest pure gold nugget in the district was recovered on this creek in 1913 when a gigantic 73 ounce piece was found. Although dwarfed by the "West," an 83 ounce 5 dwt. specimen found on Spruce creek in 1899, the latter was composed of gold with some quartz, thus making the Birch creek piece the record

An open stagecoach in front of the Hotel Russell in Atlin around the turn of the century. The stage ran between Atlin and Lake Surprise.

all-gold nugget ever found in the area.

Prospects: Perhaps not as good as some of the other placer creeks in the area although there are some Atlin miners who would argue this statement. Possibilities of paying drifting operations still exist in various places on this creek and there are some areas which offer some promise to small-scale hydraulic operations.

Not generally as interesting as some of the other streams in the Atlin area.

The cemetery in Atlin, like most of the old mining town cemeteries, has wooden headboards for markers. Both Kenneth McLaren and Fritz Miller, the "Fathers of Atlin Camp," lie buried here.

Boulder Creek - Also discovered in 1898, Boulder creek enters Lake Surprise from the north side just west of Ruby creek. Although it was exceptionally rich for one mile of its length it gained a reputation for "spotiness" but despite this it was worked from the discovery year onwards almost continuously. The section worked earliest ranged from "23 Below" to "20 Above" the original Discovery Claim.

The yield from this creek was surprisingly high, of all the Atlin placer streams it ranks third in total production, exceeded only by Spruce and Pine creeks. It was also noted for its unusually deep hard-pan which proved so tenacious and difficult to penetrate that it often required blasting to pass it.

Boulder has been hydraulicked extensively and even gigantic names like the Consolidated Mining and Smelting Company have tackled it - and not always successfully, despite its richness. The gold is comparable in fineness to both Wright and Pine creeks, which is the finest in the

region. The size is coarse with the majority of nuggets found prior
to 1900. An interesting piece recovered in 1899 weighed in at 19 ounces
3 pennyweight. Evidently hundreds of large nuggets were recovered from
Boulder in the early days of mining on the creek.

Prospects: A difficult creek to assess. Even experienced hands who
are familiar with this creek hesitate to project the chances of success.
All sorts of problems have to be overcome; the deep overburden, tough
hard-pan, the size of the boulders encountered and poor tailings grades
are just a few of the difficulties.

Although it was a formidable producer of placer gold, the general
concensus of opinion is that Boulder is not as promising as some of
the other placer creeks in the Atlin district.

A dog team in front of a miner's cabin on McKee creek - circa 1900.

McKee Creek - Flowing into Atlin Lake from the east side, McKee lies
about 8 miles south of Atlin town. Although only about 7 miles in length
it eventually produced more gold than any other stream in the region,
with the exception of Spruce and Pine creeks.

Discovered in 1898, it was heavily worked, first by the usual old
hand-mining methods and, by the turn of the century, by extensive and
generally profitable hydraulic operations run by outfits like the Atlin
Mining Company and a number of others.

The usual coarse gold was recovered along with many nuggets, one
of the largest being a 28 ounce 15 pennyweight piece. It proved to be
a consistent producer right through to the thirties when individuals

like George Adams were still obtaining good results.

The old channel of McKee has in the past been noted for its rich "pay" and a large percentage of the returns came from this channel. A noted drawback on McKee creek was the presence of large boulders which hindered mining.

Prospects: Probably good in sections where earlier mining was not carefully planned or executed. It has been hydraulicked a great deal but its record over the years is enviable. There are still some areas where sniping might return some results and a few places which could be drifted.

Atlin miners blowing black-sand off the gold. Pokes of gold-dust and a set of gold scales may be seen on the table. This was a laborious way of separating the black-sand from the gold although this method is still in use even today. This photograph was taken in 1899.

O'Donnel River - This river flows into the east side of Atlin Lake about 14 miles south of the town of Atlin. This placer river is about 30 miles long and is the largest stream emptying into the lake. Many of its numerous tributaries also carry placer gold.

Discovered in 1898 and known then as either Moose or Caribou, it was bypassed in favour of other creeks in the region where the placer gold was coarser and more plentiful. In 1912, however, when rich "pay" was discovered on a high bench in the central section, it attracted a minor stampede. The following year considerable sluicing, drifting and hydraulicking was carried out on this ground which is located about 12½ miles from the mouth of the river. Although some operations gave good returns, an insufficiency of water for hydraulicking and a generally flat gradient prevented any real progress from being made.

Prospects: Certainly not as promising as most of the other creeks in the district but there are sections in the central area which are supposedly worth examining.

Running the hurdles at the Atlin Sports Day on the Fourth of July, 1899. Both the Queen's Birthday, the 24th of May, and the American holiday, July 4th, were celebrated in Atlin. The jubilant look on the winner's face may be because of his anticipation of the cash prize awarded to the winners of each event.   (Provincial Archives photograph)

Otter Creek – Discovered in 1898, this stream empties into the south side of Lake Surprise about 2 miles west of Wright creek. In the early years a fair-sized mining camp was situated on the banks of this creek although little remains on the site today. It is remembered primarily because of a grisly murder and subsequent manhunt which took place there in 1899.

Otter creek ranks sixth in overall production in the Atlin district and some good results were obtained on this creek in the early days, especially above the Upper Canyon. The placer gold tended to be a little finer than most of the gold from Atlin although nuggets running from

1 to 5 ounces were not uncommon. For some years the famous Compagnie Francaise des Mines d'Or du Canada tenaciously hydraulicked a number of leases along Otter, obtaining varying results.

Bed-rock is deep, especially near the mouth and this obstacle and and the large boulders encountered as well, often made work on this creek either difficult or unprofitable.

Prospects: Although probably not as good as Spruce, Ruby or Wright, there are still some interesting possibilities. Some drifting in old workings might yield returns as might sniping in selected areas.

Pine Creek - This is a gold creek with a fascinating history. It flows out of Lake Surprise and empties into Atlin Lake just south of the town of Atlin. Although only 12 miles in length, the "gold bearing" section is approximately two miles long. This historic stream was the first staked in the entire region when Fritz Miller and Kenneth McLaren staked their "Discovery Claim" in 1898 at a point just east of where the remains of once-booming "Pine City" now stand. It achieved a high reputation so quickly that by 1899 an estimated 3,000 prospectors were strung out along its banks. In short order it became renowned for its coarse gold and large nuggets, and some of the nuggets recovered from this particular creek were indeed mammoth specimens. Among the more noteworthy were pieces weighing 31 ounces 1 pennyweight, recovered in 1900, and another tilting the scales at an impressive 48 ounces 12 pennyweights, found in 1925. Altogether there were scores of nuggets weighing in excess of the 10 ounce size and thousands weighing over an ounce.

The history of Pine Creek was typical, it was first worked with rockers, then sluices and waterwheels, and when the individual miner gave way to the larger companies, hydraulicking operations came into being. Although the hydraulicking companies recovered the bulk of the placer gold taken from the creek, practically every device known to miners was used on the creek, including both dredges and steam-shovels.

The best "pay" was found on or close to bedrock and in places where this impervious layer was "irregular," which was commonplace on Pine Creek, considerable quantities of gold were recovered from cracks and crevices. Where the bedrock was well "weathered," the placer gold was found to have penetrated to some depth.

Like many creeks Pine had its irregularities. The most difficult problem encountered by both the early and later miners was the presence of "clay-cemented" gravel, a gravel which proved so hard that a high recovery of gold was practically impossible. Some areas of the creek were especially rich, the most celebrated of these was undoubtedly the stretch known as "Gold Run," an old channel just south of the present channel of Pine Creek, in which unusually high values were encountered, especially where the ancient channel intersected Pine Creek. Various other places like "Nugget Hill" were also worked and re-worked because of their richness.

Prospects: Any placer gold creek with the long and rich history of Pine cannot be bypassed. Although much of it has been thoroughly mined there are still opportunities for individuals. Much of the early mining was poorly done and there are undoubtedly places which were missed by the prospectors of three-quarters of a century ago. The best

Discovery or Pine City in its heyday. This town came into being in 1898 with the discovery of placer gold on nearby Pine Creek by Fritz Miller and Kenneth McLaren. For a few heady years it boasted a population of 1,000 and rivalled Atlin. Along its one gaudy main street the thirsty miner paused for the drink that refreshes at hotels like the Pine Tree, The Nugget, The Gold House and half a dozen others.

Some of the machinery on Spruce Creek in the Atlin district around the turn of the century. At first overshadowed by nearby Pine Creek, Spruce eventually became the premier creek in the area and to date has yielded more than $7,000,000 in placer gold.

possibilities, according to several authorities on the creek, would be to locate the extension of "Gold Run," if in fact, it actually does continue eastward toward Lake Surprise, as many are convinced it does. Other possibilities include drifting in old areas in anticipation of locating virgin paydirt, or re-working old tailings or re-shovelling worked bedrock again, a practice which has proven extremely remunerative in the past for several fortunate prospectors.

An intriguing creek.

The upper end of Discovery or Pine City in 1899 with Pine creek below. While the placer gold lasted, Pine City flourished, but when the gold played out, so did the camp, and by 1915 only a hollow town remained on the flats above the creek which had been responsible for its birth.

Ruby Creek - Discovered in 1898, Ruby creek flows into the north side of Lake Surprise about 3 miles to the east of Boulder creek. Very little work was done on this placer stream in the first few years due to several difficulties encountered. Overburden was a layer of pre-glacial lava which made mining on this creek burdensome and for some time it was neglected in favour of other and easier placer streams. Later, however, it was found that the gold was there in quantity and that the gold was extremely coarse, some miners claiming that it was even coarser than the Wright creek gold.

The results from Ruby have occasionally been spectacular with some clean-ups, even in the 1930's, yielding exceptionally good "pay." The

size of the gold is impressive and a nugget recovered on the Mason and
Schulz Lay in 1931 bears this out. On July 3rd of that year the miners
on the claim found a nugget 3⅞ inches long, 3¼ inches wide and 2⅛ inches
thick which weighed 47 ounces 13 pennyweight. This massive nugget had
apparently rolled through the sluice-boxes of a former operation.

The lava covering varies widely in thickness and seems to increase
upstream. The gravel is often baked and cemented and sometimes yields
good results when old tailings are re-worked. The bedrock is unusual
for the Atlin area in that it is granite and it is often so fractured
and weathered that experienced miners work it up to a depth of 4 feet
where it is soft, the gold having penetrated the crevices in bed-rock
to this depth.

The richest "pay" was usually found from 2 feet above bed-rock
down to that layer and in the fractures and crevices in it. During the
early thirties several two and three man operations were recovering
over 100 ounces in their two week clean-ups. This would be equivalent
to over over $30,000 in at today's prices.

Ruby creek ranks fourth in total production in the Atlin camp,
surpassed only by Spruce, Pine and Boulder creeks.

Prospects: It is generally accepted that there are places along
this creek which would pay well even today. However, the old problems
are still there - the lava overburden, cemented gravel, the location
of ancient channels and at certain periods during the season, a lack
of an adequate water supply for hydraulicking operations. The mouth of
the creek is not considered good ground as the depth of bed-rock is
far too deep and upstream the lava covering increases in depth. In the

One of the waterwheels on Spruce Creek in 1971.

The town of Discovery dying in 1915. By that year most of Pine creek's gold had been mined and the death verdict had been passed on Atlin's once formidable rival.   (Courtesy of the Atlin Museum)

past, hydraulicking the lower section and drifting farther up was the usual practice. This is a placer stream where "slugs" and nuggets are commonplace. An absolutely fascinating stream.

Ruby is still considered by many to have undeveloped potential.

Spruce Creek - A certain Fred Marius, a prospector whose background is otherwise obscure, staked this creek in 1898 near the mouth of a tributary known as Eureka creek. The first "colours" were fine and little did Marius realize that he had discovered a stream which would one day yield more placer gold than any other stream in the province except Williams and Lightning, the two greatest producers in the famous Cariboo gold-fields.

In the first few years, however, its huge potential was not apparent and the miners who tenaciously probed its gravels in search of the noble metal were invariably disappointed.

The 1899 Report of the Minister of Mines glumly summed up the creek in its opening paragraph:

"This creek has had more work done on it than any other, and with very poor results to the worker...."

And Spruce creek guarded its wealth well, as a host of problems dogged the miners - poor drainage, depth to bed-rock and cemented gravel. But they persisted and the creek slowly began to surrender its riches. In a number of places for several miles above the Discovery Claim very rich and shallow ground on the creek-bed was found. These small strikes stimulated further exploration and it gradually became evident that for almost ten miles Spruce creek was literally studded with placer gold. Soon the ground hummed with activity and new high-grade deposits continued to be found, right from the junction of the creek with Pine creek, up-stream through the canyons, including the celebrated "Blue Canyon," and beyond to the upper reaches of the creek.

Unlike almost all the other creeks in the Atlin district, Spruce did not easily lend itself to large-scale operations and it became and has remained the stronghold of the individual miner to this day. Some prospectors worked the same claim continuously and always made wages or better. Old H. G. Marshall, almost a fixture on Spruce, stayed on the same claim for more than thirty years, and there were others who did the same.

The coarse gold is usually found on or in close proximity to bed-rock although finer gold occurs in other stratas above that layer. The bed-rock itself is often heavily weathered and was usually cut into as much as 2 feet to obtain the gold which had penetrated the crevices and cracks. In some places it was not unusual to find the gold averaging as much as 20 ounces per 40 square feet of bed-rock. The nuggets from Spruce were often matchless specimens, the largest being the quartz and gold chunk found by two American miners, West and Hoffenen, in 1899 at "126 Below." It weighed an astonishing 83 ounces 5 pennyweights and was nicknamed "The West." Another recovered in 1901 tipped the scales at just over 36 ounces, and one picked up by Carl Lykergard in 1936 ran 44 ounces 3 pennyweights. As late as 1969 a 16 ounce specimen was found by an American prospector who was looking over old worked-over ground.

Despite its slow start this prolific creek eventually produced over 300,000 fine ounces of gold - valued at $7,000,000. A yield which represented an almost unbelievable 10 tons of raw gold, making it the premier producer in the district.

Prospects: Spruce creek is still probably one of the best placer creeks in the province although it has been mined continuously for a period of almost seventy-five years. In places it has been hand-mined extremely well, with extensive drifting and hydraulicking operations, but some of the early work was sloppily done and there are undoubtedly areas where good values still exist.

One old miners' theory concerning Spruce merits mention. This premise stated that wherever a clean "blue" gravel met the "yellow" gravel, high values were always encountered. Surprisingly, this was often the case, thus giving credence to the theory.

Although there are many theories and other speculations concerning this creek, it must still be considered the best creek in the area. There are few placer streams anywhere which can rival Spruce.

The "Tarahne" lying abandoned on the shores of Lake Atlin in 1971.

Squaw Creek - This placer creek has a fascinating story behind its discovery. Although it is located in the Atlin Mining Division, it is partly in the Yukon and partly in British Columbia, the lower portion lying in Yukon territory and the upper part in the province. A mere 8 miles in length it flows into the Tatshenshini River approximately 10 miles from old Dalton Post.

In 1927, almost three decades after the Atlin field had been discovered, a Klukshu Indian who went by the name of Paddy Duncan stumbled across coarse gold and nuggets on the upper reaches of Squaw creek. A cursory examination revealed that there was visible free gold, in great abundance, for several hundred yards along the waterway.

Afraid of the news leaking out the local Indians quickly staked the entire length of the creek from its mouth to its source, making it the only rich placer creek in the province controlled by Indians.

Between 1927 and 1931 the gravel was worked quietly and with some spectacular results. The word, however, eventually leaked out and by 1932 there were several parties of whites on the creek.

During the thirties it became noted for its coarse gold, the largest nugget recorded on this creek weighed a hefty 46 ounces 5 pennyweight and was found in 1937. In 1931 and 1932 nuggets valued at $130, $162 and $216 were found, as well as numerous smaller pieces. Although total production from this creek reportedly did not exceed $150,000 it was a creek in which hundreds of "slugs" of gold, ranging from $3 to $20 and upwards were found.

Most of the early work was done above the "Discovery Claim" and the boulders encountered by the miners were absolutely amazing, some of them ran up to 10 feet in diameter and made the hand-mining methods extremely burdensome.

The bed-rock was invariably shallow and almost all of the gold was found on that layer. The early returns were often exceptional, in one day's clean-up, three Indians, Drury Crow, Harry Joe and Jimmy Kudwat, realized a total of $291.90 for their day's labour, pretty good wages for the dirty thirties.

Prospects: The history of this creek is intriguing but the gold deposits were located on shallow ground and undoubtedly it has been virtually exhausted, although there may be places remaining where the Indians, in their excitement over the large nuggets, passed over ground which contained paydirt.

An interesting creek.

Wright Creek - This creek flows into the south side of Lake Surprise and is located about 2 miles to the east of Otter creek. Although the majority of the Atlin placer creeks carried coarse gold, Wright creek was exceptional and surpassed all the other creeks in this respect. Many notable nuggets came from this creek and one fine sample, found in 1899 and exhibited at the Paris Exposition in 1900, weighed 25 ounces ½ pennyweight.

Around the turn of the century Wright creek was considered one of the most promising creeks in the area and paid much better, in proportion to the number of claims worked, than any other stream in the region, including Pine creek. At that time most of the results were obtained from the claims lying between "19 Below" and "48 Above" the Discovery Claim. Overshot wheels and deep shafts, some running to bed-rock at 60 feet, were in operation even then, as well as extensive hydraulicking.

The bed-rock increases in depth below the original Discovery Claim and the old channel generally conforms to the present valley although there are several places where it wanders slightly.

Over the years Wright has been worked extensively by miners like the Nord brothers, John Hyland, J. E. Moran, L. T. Hodges and a number of others. Generally these operations included drifting, shovelling-in, ground-sluicing and hydraulicking.

Prospects: Wright creek deserves serious consideration as past reports indicate that some high-grade deposits remain. The purity of the placer gold is amongst the highest in the region and it is also probably the coarsest. A close analysis of the old mining reports is undoubtedly necessary if good prospects are to be found. Although it is not as easy to reach as some of the other Atlin creeks; because of this factor it may be one of the best creeks remaining in the district.

Certainly worth examining.

Several boarded-up buildings in Atlin in 1971.

CONCLUSION

Don't miss Atlin, it is still almost unspoiled and the scenery is nothing short of spectacular. History still lingers along the placer creeks where the argonauts of yesterday toiled for the precious metal. Even now there are prospectors who, faithfully each season, snipe in the old tailings or drift for virgin paydirt in the hopes of finding another Eldorado in this historic area.

This is the north at its best, you won't be disappointed in this area they call – the Atlin country.

VII
CASSIAR

8

(43)

INTRODUCTION

The Stikine River area has been included under the general heading "Cassiar" because of the close geographical and historical connections between the two regions.

Placer gold was first discovered in the general area in 1861 when the bars of the Stikine were found to be gold-bearing. Some of these bars, mainly between the Chutine River and Telegraph Creek, were worked for years with generally good returns. A few like Rich Bar and Buck's Bar proved to be consistent producers.

It was also found that placer gold in diminishing quantities was recovered farther up the Stikine – an indicator that the source was yet to be found, but it remained for two strangers from the far Mackenzie to make the great discoveries in the Cassiar country. These two wanderers were Angus McCulloch and Henry Thibert.

Little is known about McCulloch, whose end came tragically soon after his appearance in the region, but some of his movements have been traced. It is recorded that he had taken part in the hectic gold rush to the Big Bend country in southern British Columbia prior to his appearance in the north, where in the fall of 1870 he was prospecting in the Mackenzie River district. While there he met Henry Thibert and

A forgetful prospector with his burro leaving Telegraph Creek in 1898.

his partner, a certain Henry Nakingus. Thibert, a French-Canadian from Montreal, had moved to St. Paul, Minnesota, and had drifted west from there, prospecting as he went. When Nakingus returned east the next spring, Thibert, without a partner, joined forces with Angus McCulloch. It was a fateful decision; each was an experienced prospector and both had a feeling, almost a premonition, about the virtually unexplored country of northern British Columbia. They were convinced that somewhere in that trackless territory lay undisclosed riches - and history was to prove them right!

Together they struck westward along the Liard where they wintered. Early in the spring of 1872 they struck "good pay" on McCulloch's Bar. Most prospectors would have stayed on to mine the bar but they pushed on and then made what was to eventually prove to be their most momentuous choice - they turned southward and headed for the Stikine. Ascending the Dease River, they passed by Dease Lake and soon after arrived at Buck's Bar on the Stikine. It is not certain whether or not Thibert and Angus McCulloch actually discovered gold in one of the creeks flowing into Dease Lake, but they may have found definite signs, for McCulloch soon after left for Victoria where he attempted unsuccessfully to interest the provincial government in providing funds for further prospecting in the region.

The unfortunate McCulloch, on his way back from Victoria to rejoin Thibert, was trapped in a howling snowstorm and froze to death on the banks of the Stikine River below Buck's Bar - fate had intervened and

The North West Mounted Police headquarters in Glenora, B. C. in 1898. From the left are:J. Lumsden, Malcolm MacLean, F. Waldron and D. Todd.

thus McCulloch, that intrepid explorer who had experienced hardships and hunger died a few short miles from refuge, destined never to see or participate in the golden era of the Cassiar, the region which he had helped discover.

Thibert, upon hearing of his partner's death, then set out with two other French-Canadians from Buck's Bar and headed for Dease Lake. It was April of 1873. A month later, on the western side of Dease Lake they struck pay-dirt in almost unbelievable amounts on a stream which later became known as "Thibert," after the leader of the expedition. It was an auspicious start - the first of many strikes in the region called "The Cassiar."

The returns from Thibert Creek were amazing, much of the gold lay on bedrock which was a mere 18 inches under the gravel and in places the gold went up to 3 ounces per pan.

The little band fashioned crude rockers and until the end of May they averaged 4 ounces of gold per day each. In the early part of June they made a wingdam at the mouth of the creek and for ten weeks they extracted anywhere from 5 to 11 ounces of gold per day for each hand. In days when an ordinary labourer was making about $25 a month - each of the miners was averaging nearly $125 per day and making almost one year's pay in two days.

Soon after, Captain "Billy" Moore, of sternwheeler fame, and his two sons, John and William, penetrated the area and struck rich "pay" on another creek south of Thibert. "Dease" Creek had been discovered, and it too proved immensely rich.

An 1898 pack train heading out into the north country.

By late summer of 1873 twenty miners, mainly from Buck's Bar, were hard at work and making almost $50 per day to the hand. News of the new strike; despite the efforts of old hands to keep it quiet, spread like wildfire, first to the Omineca and then to the Cariboo, but it was too late in the season for the miners in those regions to start for the distant Cassiar so they waited impatiently for spring.

With the spring of 1874 came a flood of new miners, and Laketown, or Laketon, as it was later known came into being. A typical mining camp situated at the mouth of Dease Creek it was to be the springboard to other finds in the region.

With a population of 1,600 miners, Thibert and Dease creeks were soon completely staked and those without good diggings began fanning out to locate other placer creeks.

In the summer of 1874 the redoubtable Henry McDame, a coloured prospector who had always been in the vanguard in exploring beyond the frontier, discovered another fabulous creek. This creek, soon called "McDame," was to ultimately become the greatest placer gold stream in the region and was to yield a total of $1,500,000 in the first twenty years after its discovery. Located nearly 90 miles north of Dease Lake, it soon became apparent that supplies could not be packed all the way from Laketown. So, to accommodate the McDame Creek miners, a new camp called "Centreville" came to life.

Photographed by R. Maynard.

73 ounces of gold! This is a photograph of the McDame Creek nugget which was found in 1877 by one Alfred Freeman. The original nugget was actually somewhat larger than it appears in the picture and was reputed to be the largest all-gold nugget ever recovered in British Columbia.

THE CASSIAR REGION

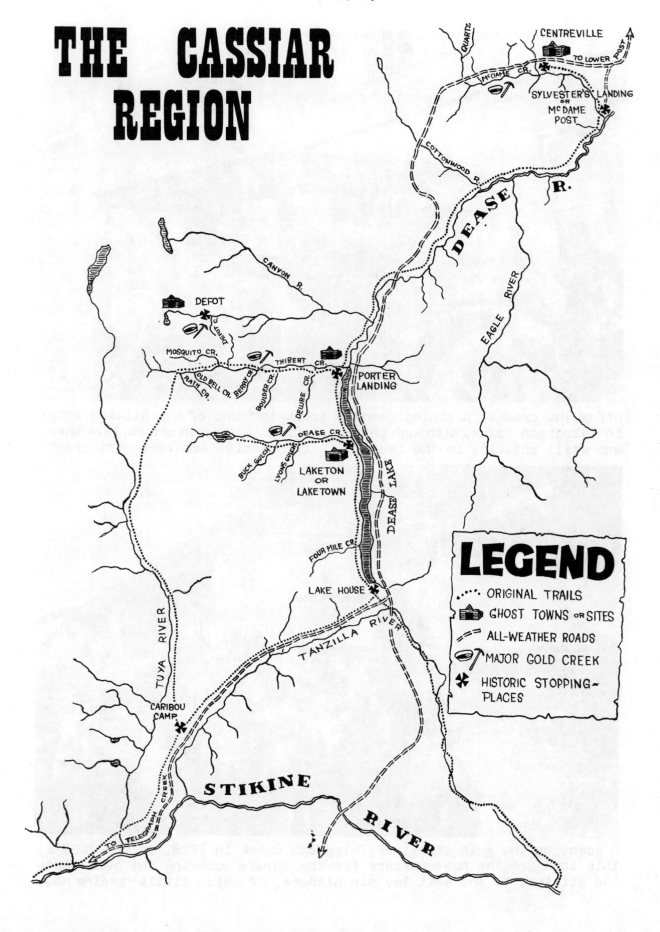

LEGEND
····· ORIGINAL TRAILS
🏚 GHOST TOWNS or SITES
╌╌ ALL-WEATHER ROADS
⛏ MAJOR GOLD CREEK
✳ HISTORIC STOPPING-PLACES

Off to the creeks! A mining company truck in front of the Stikine Hotel in Telegraph Creek. Although this photograph was taken around 1924 there was still activity in the region.   (Provincial Archives Photograph)

A scene on the main street of Telegraph Creek in 1928. In the 1860's, this town was the headquarters for the miners working the bars along the Stikine. To the east lay old Glenora, of which little remains now.

Centreville was not unlike Laketown although even in its heyday in the mid-1870's its population never rose above 300. Like other camps its permanent residents included the usual array of store-owners and saloon-keepers as well as a handful of "tinhorn" gamblers. It was a rough town where any differences of opinion were generally decided by "knock-down" brawls; and the store-owners, an unusually avaricious lot, charged all that the traffic would bear, a "Square meal" of bread, beans and black coffee going for a prohibitive $2.00, and their other prices were not far behind. The saloon-keepers, not to be outdone, hawked their wares, well-watered drinks, at 25¢ each. It was a camp where few of the miners tarried for very few men left the Cassiar with a stake if they dallied too long in Centreville, for if the store-owners or saloon-keepers didn't take them, the gamblers did.

From 1874 to 1877, the "Big Three" of the Cassiar; Dease, Thibert and McDame produced $891,600, $863,400 and $808,500 respectively, for a total of more than $2,500,000 in four brief years. Strangely, up to 1877 there was little production from any other placer creeks, but as the yield from the major producers and their tributaries began to wane the prospectors fanned out to find new creeks.

In the summer of 1878, John Defot and a brother of Henry Thibert known as Thibert Jr., accompanied by several other French-Canadians, travelled down the Dease River and turned west when they came to the Canyon River. Seven miles up that river it forked and the little band chose the west fork and followed it for almost 13 more miles, panning each tributary as they moved up-river. The results, however, were less than encouraging as "colours," that faithful indicator of gold, were hard to come by. Tired and discouraged most of the miners wanted to return to Thibert Creek but urged on by Defot they agreed to "try" one more

A biplane at Dease Lake - circa 1924.

creek before they turned back.

The next tributary, an insignificant looking stream flowing out of a little valley to the south, appeared disenchanting. Fully expecting it to be as barren as the previous creeks the downhearted prospectors nevertheless began to wash its gravels. Moments later Defot jumped up and held aloft a glittering piece of metal - gold! The nugget triggered the miners into action and within minutes it was obvious that they had struck prodigiously rich diggings. Thus another Cassiar placer creek came into being - and they named it "Defot."

There were other creeks like French, Walker, and many more but compared to Dease, Thibert, McDame and Defot their production was insignificant. In later years a few more gold creeks were found and one of them called Wheaton, or Boulder, as it was originally known, caused considerable excitement for a short time when it was found to carry coarse gold.

But the early years in the Cassiar were the great years, times when Laketown, Porter Landing and Centreville were going concerns, when 1,600 miners gleaned the gravels of its creeks in their never ending search for "paydirt."

Now most of the "diggings" of yesterday are exhausted and the mining camps of a hundred years ago are no more, but the region is still compelling, the vastness of the area, like much of the north, lends it a grandeur not felt in more southerly regions. "Cassiar" still has a lure, especially for those who love the back-country of British Columbia.

The remains of old Glenora in 1912.

THE PLACER CREEKS

● Thibert Creek - This was the first placer gold creek located in the Cassiar. Lying on the western side of Dease Lake, this stream flows into that body of water at the north end. Discovered in April, 1873, by Henry Thibert and several other French-Canadians, it initiated the rush into the Cassiar.

   Initially, the gold was found to be in shallow deposits and the first returns were so astonishing that earnings of $100 per day per man were commonplace.

   Like many of the creeks in this region the gold was exceedingly coarse and nuggets up to 18 ounces were reported. The lower portion of the creek paid anywhere from 1 to 3 ounces per man through most of the 1870's. The upper part of the creek was "spotted" and although much promise was indicated in certain sections on the upper creek, most of the production came from the lower section.

   The official returns from Thibert from 1874 through to 1895 were $1,279,600. The first year was the banner year and $400,000 was taken then. The production gradually declined thereafter.

   The creek was extensively hand-mined at first by both white and

Curtis and Tulk's Store in Telegraph Creek in 1898. In this year there was a renewal of placer mining activity along the Stikine. Later, many of the prospectors continued on to the Atlin or Yukon goldfields.

Chinese. The Chinese made their appearance in the Cassiar shortly after its discovery. Some whites, in an effort to discourage the influx of Oriental miners, erected warning notices along the trails leading into the Cassiar and in the spring of 1874, a Chinese headman vanished while en route to the Cassiar from Buck's Bar. Whether his disappearance was actually murder or not has never been determined. In any event, the Chinese continued to come into the district in ever increasing numbers. By 1880, the production of the various creeks was falling off and the Chinese by then comprised over half of the mining population and owned the majority of the claims.

By that date Thibert Creek had also passed its peak and the old original miners, many of them colourful characters like Nememiah T. Smith, commonly known as "Black Jack," had left for other areas. And by 1895, barely a dozen men, mostly Chinese, were still at work on the creek and although it was later hydraulicked with somewhat indifferent results by the turn of the century it was generally considered to be "worked out."

Prospects: Because of its reputation for "spotiness" it is still a reasonable bet for novice panners. There are areas which have been lightly prospected in the past and these places still warrant a look today. The chances of locating small, high-grade deposits of "pay-dirt" are possible.

Quite a creek and quite a history.

Waiting for the sternwheeler in old Glenora in 1898. Glenora was the head of navigation on the Stikine and was as far as the sternwheelers dared to go. From this point the supplies were packed in to the upper river and the Cassiar country.   (photo - Canada West Copyright)

● <u>Dease Creek</u> - When Henry Thibert and his French-Canadian companions waded through this creek on their way to stake Thibert Creek in 1873 they unwittingly bypassed a stream which ultimately yielded nearly $1,500,000.00 in placer gold. This creek eventually ranked second only to McDame Creek in total returns from the Cassiar district.

This stream flows into the west side of Dease Lake and was first staked in 1873 by the Moores; William J., a character often referred to as "The Flying Dutchman," by profession a sternwheeler captain, and his two sons, William and John. Their "Discovery Claim" yielded great returns for some time. In the 1874 season it averaged 200 ounces per week and in one three day stretch they recovered $2,600.00 in gold.

In its heyday Dease was staked from its mouth up-stream for almost 16 miles and in 1874 supported, and supported well, a total population of 700 miners. Using the most primitive of methods a number of mining companies like the Three to One, Perseverance, Canadian, Caledonia and Baronovitch took out hundreds of dollars in gold each day. In a single working day one outfit washed a total of 135 ounces of dust and there were hundreds of companies washing anywhere from 3 to 10 and sometimes more, per day.

Mining the creek by wing-damming and rocking, the total yield for the first five years was an astounding $1,054,400.00. The placer gold was very coarse and nuggets, especially in the first years, plentiful. In 1874 a piece of gold weighing 40 ounces was found and the following year another nugget, this one weighing 50 ounces was recovered.

By 1876 the Chinese began to move in on Dease in force and were in control of most of the creek claims two years later although a few whites were still working the benches. By the year 1880 the yield had

The original courthouse at Laketon, the metropolis of the Cassiar in the 1870's. At its height Laketon had several hotels, a dozen stores, four saloons, a courthouse, a jail and nearly eighty miners' cabins. There were other rivals like Porter Landing and Centreville, but with a shifting population of almost 500 Laketon remained as the undisputed capitol of the Cassiar country.

slipped to barely $60,000.00 and the creek was considered to be mined-out.

There were probably more characters on this creek than any other in the district, as well as "The Flying Dutchman" there was a host of others including "Black Jack" Smith, "Peter the Great" Cargotitch and the celebrated "Dancing Bill" Latham, the latter a long-time friend of "Black Jack" Smith, with whom he had a long standing rivalry which ended only when Latham died in 1880. His final words were that he "did not really mind dying but regretted that he could not outlive 'Black Jack.'" They were a strange lot but they had good company.

By the turn of the century Dease Creek had been almost abandoned and Laketown, a populous "city" in the hectic 1870's, lay deserted, destined to become yet another in a long list of "ghost towns," towns whose fate had been decided by the shifting fortunes of gold.

Prospects: Probably as good as Thibert although Dease Creek had a longer stretch of "paying" creek. It was extensively worked in the early years but there are still a few places where values remain. The best bet may be to re-work old ground which was carelessly worked in the 1870's. It is still considered worthwhile panning in spots.

Not a promising creek but interesting.

The last remaining structure of the H. B. Co.'s post at Sylvester's Landing in 1971. The miners bought their provisions here before heading up the trail to McDame Creek and the rich diggings found by Henry McDame on that creek in 1874. This part of the Cassiar country still has an almost eerie atmosphere - a place where the echoes from yesterday are almost audible.

● <u>McDame Creek</u> - The history of this creek is so incredible that it almost sounds like a dime novel. It is undeniably the most interesting and probably the most unpredictable gold creek in the Cassiar.

Even its discovery was unique. In the summer of 1874, one Henry McDame, a coloured prospector who had been on the Fraser in 1858 and had later been one of the first miners into Germansen Creek in the Omineca, was prospecting almost 100 miles north of Dease Lake. Like all experienced prospectors he panned each creek he came to. Finally, on one of the tributaries of the Dease River he found interesting "colours." Following the stream into the mountains he noted that the gold was becoming increasingly more abundant, sensing that he was on the verge of a strike, he doggedly continued up-stream. His tenacity paid off for at a spot nearly 15 miles from its mouth he came across rich "pay" on bedrock. It was another strike!

Returning immediately to Laketown he formed a company with eight other miners and called it the Charity Company. Making their way back to the stream they staked their Discovery Claims, then wingdammed the creek and began washing gold. In their first month of mining they took out $6,000 in coarse gold.

As usual the word spread quickly and before the summer was out hundreds of claims had been staked and in the gulch near where McDame had made his discovery, a rough town began to take shape. Later, this crude camp became known as "Centreville."

1875 was ushered in with great hopes but it was soon to prove to be disappointing. The creek, like so many others in the Cassiar, was

Miners lounging in front of Shaw and Tomlinson's Store in Glenora in 1898. Notice the sleds behind the prospector in the foreground.

"spotted," and rich ground much scarcer than had been anticipated. In spite of this, the total production for the year edged to the $300,000 mark.

Some tributaries like Trout, Quartz and especially Snow gave good results. On the latter creek, the Discovery Company, made up of four old Cariboo veterans; Sylvester, Black, Christie and the inimitable Vital Laforce of Omineca fame, struck a lead which eventually proved to be the richest ever uncovered in the Cassiar. During most of 1876 the company followed the lead which soon became known as the "Christie Lead," and in so doing they recovered returns ranging from $2,000.00 to $6,000.00 each week. The next year they managed to continue mining the lead by obtaining bench claims in line with the original lead and were able to stay with it by "hydraulicking and tunnelling" into the side-hill between Quartz Creek and Snow Creek. The amount and size of the gold found in the operations was astounding - there were countless numbers of nuggets running anywhere from 1 to 8 ounces and the rest of the gold was almost uniformly coarse. Eventually, however, the company lost the lead and unable to find it again, they suspended operations. In the next few years, numerous other outfits attempted to re-locate the "Lost Christie Lead" but none succeeded - the lottery of gold had chosen to pass them by.

It was also in 1877 that the attention of miners everywhere in the province was drawn to McDame Creek because of an occurrence which captured their imaginations. In the spring of that year, a miner named Alfred Freeman, while sluicing on the Discovery Company's claim near Centreville, washed out what at first appeared to be a boulder. Because of its size he threw it aside, but in so doing was impressed by its great weight. Curious, he retrieved "the boulder" and to his utter and

The Gold Commissioner's Office at Centreville on McDame Creek as it appeared in 1928.   (Provincial Archives photograph)

complete amazement it proved to be a massive gold nugget weighing 73 ounces. It was the largest nugget ever found in British Columbia.

For seven consecutive years McDame produced between $100,000 and $300,000 annually but by 1881 it had begun to slip, when for the first time, the yield fell under $100,000. By that date most of the claims were in the hands of the Chinese and as the years wore on the yield continued to decline until it was averaging under $10,000 per year by the early 1890's. McDame Creek, the mightiest placer gold producer in the Cassiar, was effectively mined out.

Prospects: McDame, with its 16 miles of pay creek is still worth looking at. There are several places between old Cantreville and the junction of Quartz and Trout Creeks which present possibilities even today. This is an area which still has a "feel" of history and of the past. It is worth panning in selected locations and could even yield reasonable "pay" in a few rare places on the upper reaches.

A creek worth investigating.

● Defot Creek – This was the fourth ranking producer in the entire area and was discovered later than any of the other three major placer gold creeks.

A tributary of the west fork of the Canyon River and north-west of Dease Lake, it came into prominence in 1878 when John Defot and a party of French-Canadians located rich "pay" there. Two hundred miners stampeded into the new region and almost overnight several stores and two saloons appeared as a new mining camp called "Defot" came to life. Working feverishly the miners quickly turned the little valley into a

A one ounce nugget, a brass and iron lock and several Chinese coins found by a prospector at Centreville in 1971.

cauldron of activity as wingdams and sluices were erected. At first this stream yielded good returns and Thibert Jr., who sold his share of the Discovery Claim for a paltry $500, was dismayed to learn that the buyer had cleaned up more than that amount by the night of the purchase. Miners were making from $25 to $50 daily and large nuggets were the order of the day, a number of them weighing between 2 and 15 ounces with the largest running 45 ounces. But it was short-lived, by 1880 there were barely 40 miners remaining on the creek and the returns had slid to $15,000 from $95,000 the year before. Strangely, none of the creeks nearby yielded any significant quantities of gold.

Prospects: Defot's total length was worked assiduously and chances of missed paydirt are slender indeed. There was a time when this stream knew heady days but those years are long gone.

Gold Pan Creek - A small tributary of the Little Eagle River about 10 miles east of Dease Lake. Discovered in the fall of 1925 by two partners named Grady and Ford, who found coarse gold on rim-rock near the mouth of the creek, their find touched off a rush and by the end of the year 165 claims had been staked on Gold Pan and tributary creeks. In the summer of 1925 more than 400 ounces of nuggety gold was recovered, 242 ounces from Grady and Ford's "Discovery" claim.

The bedrock on many parts of the creek was shallow and fairly easy to mine. Hand-sluiced in the early years it was later mined extensively, in some sections. Dome Creek and some other tributaries were also placer producers. For almost a decade between 200 and 500 ounces were produced in the immediate area.

Still interesting prospecting country.

CONCLUSION

A few areas are steeped in mining tradition and the Cassiar is one of them. Although the old gold towns like Laketon, Centreville and Defot have now almost vanished, there are still places where the vagabond can catch glimpses of the past. On any of the trinity of creeks: Thibert or Dease or McDame, touches of those years remain, decaying cabins, piles of tailings, caved-in shafts and abandoned equipment.

Yes, those man of the past have gone too, the French-Canadians like "Buck" Choquette, Henry Thibert, Jean Defot and Vital Laforce and their English-speaking contemporaries like the irrepressible Peter Cargotitch, "Dancing Bill" Latham and "Black Jack" Smith. There were others too who became legends in their own time, miners like Henry McDame, the black who followed the will-o-the-wisp to his dying day, a man who was always beyond the fringe of the frontier, a mine-finder, a man with the Midas Touch. He was there in 1870 when Germansen Creek of Omineca fame was discovered, he was the first to strike gold on the most renowned placer creek in Cassiar, a stream which still bears his name.

Now only their exploits and their names remain, but the "Cassiar" is still much the same. In this limitless region one can still gaze into the windows of yesterday, a yesterday when hundreds of prospectors streamed into an unknown area in search of the yellow metal and El Dorado creeks.

Linger in the Cassiar - it has a special mood.

VII

OMINECA

INTRODUCTION

Omineca - It was rumoured as early as 1864 that there were gold-bearing creeks in the wilderness north-east of old Hazelton but it was not until the spring of 1869 that there were any serious attempts to exploit these finds.

When two Omineca pioneers, Michael Byrnes and Vital Laforce, made their appearance in Quesnel early that spring and brought with them tales of untouched placer creeks in the "Omineca" it elucidated great interest in that town. With the output from the famous Cariboo goldfields beginning to wane, the merchants and miners of Quesnel were most anxious to find other placer areas. These hints of a possible new goldfield in the north resulted in the starting of a public subscription to outfit a party of prospectors to explore the area. The money was quickly raised and a band of six experienced prospectors was chosen. This group, led by Michael Byrnes and accompanied by Vital Laforce, William Humphreys, Patrick Kelly, Allan Grant and James Hawkins was dubbed, "The Peace River Prospecting Party." In return for the financial assistance provided by the townspeople of Quesnel, the prospectors agreed to report all significant discoveries to their backers in Quesnel. Completely outfitted and with the good wishes of the residents of the town still ringing in their ears, the expedition left Quesnel in the early part of May, 1869, to determine whether or not the creeks of the distant "Omineca" held promise.

Spring passed and summer arrived and it stretched on into fall, and still no reports had been received from the missing prospecting party, although disquieting rumours had reached the residents of the

An old Indian chief at
Hazelton - circa 1900.
This Indian was there
when the strikes in the
Omineca were made in the
early years.

town that the miners had struck a rich creek, and contrary to the prior
agreement, were not about to disclose its location to their backers.
    Finally the miners returned, carrying reports which were highly
unfavourable. Their statements, however, were received with more than
a little suspicion, and when William Humphreys, one of the members of
the expedition, deposited 70 ounces of gold - gold which was definitely
not Cariboo gold, in the assay office in Quesnel, the suspicions turned
to outright disbelief. These feelings were fortified further when the
party bought new provisions and prepared to set out again on "another"
prospecting trip into the north. This time, however, they were followed
and overtaken on the trail by other miners from Quesnel. Finally Byrnes
and his companions turned to face their accusers, and realizing that

Omineca Street in old Hazelton in 1900. Hazelton served as the jumping-off place for many of the miners heading into the Manson Creek area.

Some decaying miners' cabins on Vital Creek - circa 1920.

any further attempts to deceive them would not only be futile but
also possibly dangerous, admitted that they had discovered a creek
in the "Omineca" which they called "Vital" Creek, after the miner
who had found it, Vital Laforce. They had, he went on, extracted a
total of $8,000 in gold from it in a span of 35 days.

After receiving assurance that the "originals" would be given
priority in the staking of claims, Byrnes led the combined group to
Silver Creek, a tributary of the Omineca River, and on the west side
of that stream about three miles from its mouth they came across a
feeder stream - Vital Creek. As they drove their claim-stakes home,
the Rush to the Omineca was inaugurated.

Vital, however, was to prove disappointing so the miners soon
began looking about for other gold creeks. The neighbouring streams
were tested and it was found that both Silver and Byrnes gave some
returns.

In 1870, more prospectors poured into the area and the quest
for new placer creeks quickened. Then, in July of that year, James
Germansen and three other prospectors, while panning a creek almost
40 miles east of Vital Creek, came across coarse gold. And a great
placer creek was born - and they called it "Germansen." It was to
become one of the heaviest producers in the entire area. A mining
camp variously known as Arctic City, Omineca City or Germansen soon
made its appearance. It was a compact and typical mining camp with
about twenty log cabins and several make-shift stores and saloons.
By that fall a total of $55,000 in gold, much of it coarse, had been
recovered from the diggings nearby.

Manson Creek as it appeared in 1913.

The following summer another strike was made, this time on Manson Creek, south of Germansen, when on July 5, 1871, Robert Howell, a former Royal Engineer, hit exceedingly coarse gold. As the miners rushed into this new bonanza it was found that many of the creeks close by, like Slate, Nugget and Lost and Black Jack Gulch also carried gold.

The rockers and sluices were soon operating and the early returns were excellent. That wandering prospector of Cariboo renown, "Twelve Foot" Davis, with his usual unerring good fortune, mined a total of 140 ounces in a single week and a number of others in the area were averaging almost 100 ounces a week.

The entire area was booming in 1871 for that year was the height of the Omineca Rush with an estimated 1,200 miners on its creeks. In Germansen City and Manson Creek wily entrepreneurs were demanding outrageous prices for the basic necessities of life. Everything was high in the region that year - the famous "Omineca Express," a simple one man operation of R. J. Lamont, the sole agent for both Wells, Fargo and Company and Barnard's Express, charged and received no less than $2.50 for each letter received. A man's wages for a day elsewhere.

It soon became apparent that the gold creeks were restricted to an area barely 15 miles deep and 55 miles across; from Vital and Silver creeks in the west to the Germansen-Manson section in the east. By the end of August the bulk of the miners, unwilling to pay the prices for supplies and facing the dreaded Omineca winter, began to pull out. When winter came only a handful of men remained to face it.

The returns from the area remained fairly high for several years but after 1871 the Omineca was never again to experience the roaring

Four Manson Creek miners in 1913, with the remains of the town in the background.   (Provincial Archives photograph)

excitement of that year when creek after creek came into production and anything less than "an ounce a day" was scoffed at.

With the discovery of the rich Cassiar goldfield in 1873, the majority of the Omineca miners were drawn away and for several years after the creeks lay in the doldrums, worked only by a persevering few. Finally, in the late 1870s, some of the miners began straggling back and for a few years thereafter intermittent production kept the region alive, but the halcyon days of 1871 were gone and were never again to be repeated.

THE PLACER CREEKS

<u>Germansen River</u> - Originally called Germansen Creek, it was found to contain coarse gold in 1870 by a party consisting of J. Germansen, Martin, May and Smith. Flowing into the Omineca River from the south at Germansen's Landing, this river has been one of the two greatest placer gold producers in the area with a probable production of about $500,000, and perhaps somewhat more.

Germansen City, which was also known as Arctic City, was located on this river in the glory years. The gold has a reputation as being

A horse race on Sports Day in South Fort George, July 1, 1912.

coarse and several nuggets seem to substantiate this; a 27 ounce gold and quartz nugget was found by the Craton Company in 1870 and in 1934 a hydraulic operation turned up a 24 ounce specimen. Slugs and smaller nuggets were commonplace.

The river has been heavily mined by all the old hand-mining methods and later operation included extensive hydraulicking by a number of Chinese companies like the Ah Lock Company.

Prospects: Like almost all of the good gold rivers Germansen has been well gone over by generations of experienced miners, both whites and Chinese. There may yet be some possibilities in old ground which was not expertly cleaned in the early years. The chances, however, of reasonable deposits of "pay-dirt" are somewhat remote.

● Lorne Creek - This placer creek flows into the Skeena River from the west and is located between Terrace and Hazelton, approximately 3 miles nprth of Doreen. The illustrious coloured miner, Henry McDame, was the first to find gold on this creek in the year 1884. In the first four years after discovery nearly $50,000 was recovered and another $25,000 since then. The largest nugget on record weighed 1½ ounces, found in 1931. Generally the gold is much finer than the Vital-Manson area.

Prospects: There are parts of the old channel which evidently have not been worked and offer some possibilities. Colours can be obtained in various spots but this creek should not be expected to return much gold today.

● Lost Creek - This creek flows into the Manson River from the south and was discovered in 1871. Its record has been surprisingly good with a reputation for nuggets and coarse gold. After the head of the canyon the "pay" ran out. It has been worked by both Chinese and whites for years.

Prospects: Certainly not as likely as Manson, Germansen or Slate but still worth examining.

Manson River - This river is located south of Germansen Landing. It was first known as Manson Creek and was discovered in 1871 by Robert Howell. It rapidly established itself as one of the two most prolific placer streams in the Omineca. Like Germansen and most of the other placer creeks in the vicinity, this river was renowned for its coarse gold.

It was wing-dammed and drifted heavily in the early years. Later it was hydraulicked. Again both whites and Chinese worked this river. It had several gulches and tributaries which gained some recognition as gold producers.

Prospects: Reasonable for the novice. A producer like Manson is always interesting. Snipers have been working it for years and getting occasionally good results. There are still places which could be worth drifting and sniping.

● Silver Creek - This placer stream flows from the south into the Omineca River approximately 35 miles west of Germansen Landing.

Discovered by Byrnes' "Peace River Prospecting Party" in 1869 it is a creek with several peculiarities. It was discovered that silver

GERMANSEN & MANSON AREAS in the OMINECA

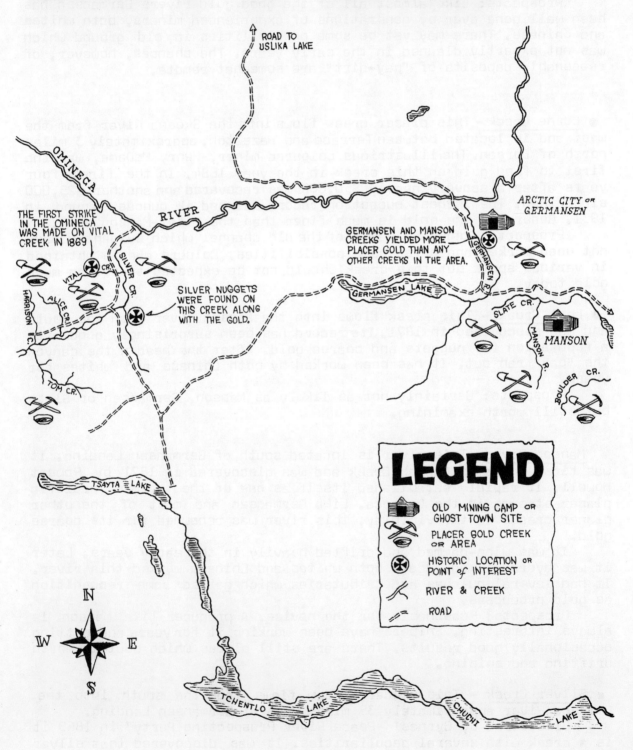

ROAD TO USLIKA LAKE

THE FIRST STRIKE IN THE OMINECA WAS MADE ON VITAL CREEK IN 1869

SILVER NUGGETS WERE FOUND ON THIS CREEK ALONG WITH THE GOLD.

GERMANSEN AND MANSON CREEKS YIELDED MORE PLACER GOLD THAN ANY OTHER CREEKS IN THE AREA.

ARCTIC CITY OR GERMANSEN

OMINECA RIVER

SILVER CR.

VITAL CR.

HARRISON R.C.

ALICE CR.

TOM CR.

GERMANSEN LAKE

GERMANSEN R.

SLATE CR.

MANSON R.

MANSON

BOULDER CR.

TSAYTA LAKE

TCHENTLO LAKE

CHUCHI LAKE

LEGEND

OLD MINING CAMP or GHOST TOWN SITE

PLACER GOLD CREEK or AREA

HISTORIC LOCATION or POINT of INTEREST

RIVER & CREEK

ROAD

nuggets, actually arquerite a native amalgam of silver, occurred along
with the gold and when the silver ceased the gold also stopped.
    The gold from this creek tends to be coarse with nuggets up to 2
ounces quite usual, especially in the years prior to 1900. It has been
well worked.
    Prospects: Again it has been mined by whites and the meticulous
Chinese and although there are various places where colours may still
be obtained, the chances of locating good "pay" are slender.

● Slate Creek - This creek is a tributary of the Manson River and flows
into that river from the west. It was also discovered in 1871 and gave
up much coarse gold and nuggets. It was wing-dammed and hand-mined to
a considerable degree.
    Prospects: Snipers have been gleaning gold from bedrock on this
gold creek for decades and some of them made a living doing it. There
were prospectors who preferred Slate to any of the other creeks in the
Omineca. There are still places which could yield some returns.

● Tom Creek - This placer stream flows out of the valley which lies
between Mt. Grant and Mt. Tom and joins Kenny Creek, a tributary of
Silver Creek, between Humphrey and Tom lakes. Discovered in 1869 by
the Byrnes Party it has yielded gold for more than one hundred years.
The gold tends towards coarseness with 1 and 2 ounce nuggets common.
Like Vital and Silver creeks, native silver nuggets also occur in this
stream.
    It has been wing-dammed, drifted and hand-mined like nearly all
the other gold creeks in the vicinity with both whites and Orientals
taking considerable gold out.
    Prospects: Several old-timers are of the opinion that Tom Creek
is one of the better creeks remaining in the vicinity. Drifting could
uncover reasonable "pay."

● Vital Creek - Found by Vital Laforce in 1869 this placer stream is
a tributary of Silver Creek and joins that creek from the west about
5 miles from its mouth. This was the first creek discovered and the
first mined in the Omineca. Native silver nuggets were also recovered
along with the gold in this creek. The gold was often coarse and well
worn with nuggets up to 2½ ounces quite common, especially before the
turn of the century.
    There was considerable hydraulicking and much deep-lead mining on
this creek, especially by Chinese syndicates like Gow Sing and Company.
These old and experienced Cariboo miners did well on this creek where
the bulk of the gold was obtained on bedrock and in the crevices and
cracks.
    Prospects: It is still a creek which warrants consideration. It
was once one of the four or five most productive placer creeks in the
Omineca and there should be at least some isolated deposits of "pay"
remaining.

● Other placer creeks in the Omineca - Sauchi, Rainbow, Harrison, Dog
and Philip and the Omineca River. In the northern region - McConnell,
Jimmay and McClair creeks. In the Lorne Creek area and elsewhere - Bob,
Buck, Kleanza, Fiddler and Porcupine creeks.

CONCLUSION

"Omineca," the word still carries a certain ring although that era when Germansen City was roaring and gold dust was changing hands nightly across its bars and gaming tables has long since passed.

The "poor man's diggings" which attracted the Cariboo miners to this remote area have lain idle for decades and the miners like "Twelve Foot" Davis, Rufus Sylvester and Michael Byrnes and their Chinese counterparts like Ah Lum and Ah Lock have vanished like the towns they once lived in.

Names like Holloway's Bar, Black Jack Gulch and Kildare Gulch attest to the fact that miners once toiled along the creeks for that precious metal. Now their workings are silent and this former center of placer activity has lapsed but that sense of history which rarely leaves a once historic area lingers on - it has in this part of the Omineca.

They say that the "deep ground" of the Germansen River still has gold in quantity and there are places remaining on Slate and Manson where experienced snipers continue to take their toll. Even today a few hopefuls still try their luck in the area, hoping to find bypassed paystreaks or a missed crevice - these are the people who understand what "the lure of the Omineca" really means.

Abandoned horses in Manson Town in 1901.

IX

PEACE RIVER

INTRODUCTION

Peace River - In 1860 rumours reached British Columbia that miners had found rich "diggings" on the Peace River. Who these prospectors were has never been determined but it is verified that in the following year two prospectors, William Cust and Edward Carey, stopped at Fort McLeod with 1,000 ounces of fine gold. They stated that they had washed the gold on the bars of the Peace and had each washed, in one day, 75 ounces.

This news soon spread and resulted in a small rush in 1862. The BRITISH COLUMBIAN of October 18, 1862, reported that the bars were paying $100 a day to miners using rockers.

In the next two years this district, which was known as Stickeen Territories then, was prospected thoroughly and although the results were discouraging - for the Peace River country is a fine gold region, several bars did yield good returns. One of bars was called Rich Bar, and the other was known as Toy's Bar. The former was located on the Peace River and the latter on the Finlay, about four miles from Finlay Forks.

These bars evidently returned anywhere from $50 to $75 per hand

A prospector rounding a nasty bend on the Peace River in 1901.
In places the Peace couldn't be run with any type of boat.

MINING GOLD
WITH A GRIZZLY

An unidentified placer miner washing gold at Branham Flats on
the Peace River in 1926.   (Provincial Archives photograph)

per day for some time. Bar diggings, however, usually play out fairly quickly and they were soon vacated for more promising regions like the Omineca and the Cassiar.

Bar-miners have worked the Peace, Finlay and Parsnip rivers for many years with varying results. This part of the province isn't really considered good "gold country," but it would have been hard to convince William Cust and Edward Carey that it wasn't in 1861.

Some fine looking Indians and a downed bear on the banks of the Peace River in 1906. The Indians, who were familiar with the country, were invariably used as guides on most of the early prospecting trips.

CONCLUSION

It is still possible to pan "colours" on some of the bars of the rivers in the Peace River country although with the completion of the hydro projects the great bar mining days have passed. The mining isn't exactly breathtaking but there remain a few spots where an experienced placer man can recover interesting quantities of the noble metal.

Although there are many better places in the province for placer mining, much of the Peace River territory is worth wandering. Far off the roads of today the trails of yesterday still beckon. In places it is almost the same as it was when the fur traders of the Hudson's Bay Company ran its rivers in their never-ending search for furs.

X

CARIBOO

The remains of Quesnel Forks in 1971. This old gold camp was the first
of the mining towns of the Cariboo. Founded in 1859 by miners streaming
up the Quesnel River following the trail of gold it ran wide open for
more than a year, but when Antler, Williams, Lightning, Cunningham and
scores of other creeks were discovered far to the north, it declined in
importance. By 1862 camps like Barkerville, Camerontown, Van Winkle and
several other towns surpassed it and Quesnel Forks began slipping. Now
this historic old camp is decaying rapidly and is in danger of vanish-
ing completely unless steps are taken to save it.

INTRODUCTION

Cariboo - The stagecoaches of the B.X. line jostling along the famous Cariboo Road, old Quesnelle Forks standing forlornly in the autumn sun, Hobson's gigantic Bullion Mine, remote Texas Ferry, a handful of gold from Little Hixon Creek, Tom Crawford, Bill Dyson, Cliff Brown, miners of today still searching for pay on the historic creeks of yesterday. These are the images of Cariboo, past and present.

And there is much more to this memorable part of British Columbia, for marching out of the mists of the past come a thousand names and a hundred places; names like "Cariboo" Cameron, "Twelve Foot" Davis, Dud Moreland, John Rose, Billy Barker, "Dutch Bill" Deitz, "Doc" Keithley and a host of others; places like Camerontown, Antler, Keithley Creek, Bullion, Van Winkle, Richfield, Barkerville, Stanley and a dozen other camps which once rang with excitement.

The name "Cariboo" conjures up visions of the greatest gold rush in the history of the province when thousands of argonauts, young and old, and from all walks of life, headed for the bonanza creeks of the Cariboo, lured by the irresistable call of gold. And gold there was, in almost unbelievable quantities.

Ingots of gold from the celebrated Bullion Mine near Likely in the Cariboo. More than a ton of gold is visible in this photograph.

Richfield in 1868

A monitor at the Bullion Mine in 1896

The vanguard of miners probing up the Quesnel and Cottonwood rivers in 1859 were unaware that they were poised on the edge of their greatest find ever - they were closing on the fabulous Cariboo.

Their efforts were especially rewarded on the banks of the Quesnel and its bars proved increasingly richer as the river was ascended. The prospectors pressed on and struck Quesnel and Cariboo lakes, again their take increased and a number of strikes on the rivers electrified the atmosphere as individual miners earned up to $100 per day. By late in the year hundreds of prospectors were encamped along the Quesnel, Cariboo and Horsefly rivers, and many of them remained, impatiently waiting for spring, as the Cariboo winter settled in.

As soon as the weather permitted in early 1860, they fanned out and soon the first of the illustrious bonanza creeks was found. It was Keithley Creek, so called after "Doc" Keithley, one of the first to find that it carried quantities of placer gold. Soon after its main tributary, Snowshoe Creek, was also found to carry gold. In short order, two more creeks farther to the north, flowing in from the west to join the Cariboo River to the north of Cariboo Lake were discovered to be gold-bearing.

These discoveries spurred on greater efforts and in the fall of 1860, John Rose, McDonald, George Weaver and "Doc" Keithley set out from Keithley Creek to prospect the unknown country to the north-west. It was to be an epic journey. Working their along and up Keithley Creek they branched off on Snowshoe and followed it to

Chinatown, Keithley Creek, 1902

Camerontown, 1868

A prospecting party on Rose's Gulch in the Cariboo near the turn of the century. Notice the tents and the sluice-boxes.

its source, continuing on they crossed the divide and descended into the little valley beyond. Below them they could see a stream and soon after they were on the upper reaches of this creek. The creek came to be called "Antler" and it was the key to the treasure chest of Cariboo.

As they struggled downstream they were amazed to find free gold lying on the bare bedrock; one pan yielded $25, another $75; the latter pan containing an almost unbelievable 4½ ounces of raw gold. They had unwittingly stumbled across an Eldorado creek - and they were the only ones in that far-flung and remote region who knew that it existed.

Their timing was fortunate for the next morning they awoke to find more than a foot of fresh snow on the ground. Shortly after they were forced to arrive at a decision, they were short of supplies and someone had to journey back to Keithley Creek for more provisions. Leaving two of the party to mine and build a log cabin the other two set off for their destination - grimly determined to keep their magnificent find a secret.

At "Red-headed" Davis's store in Keithley they casually ordered

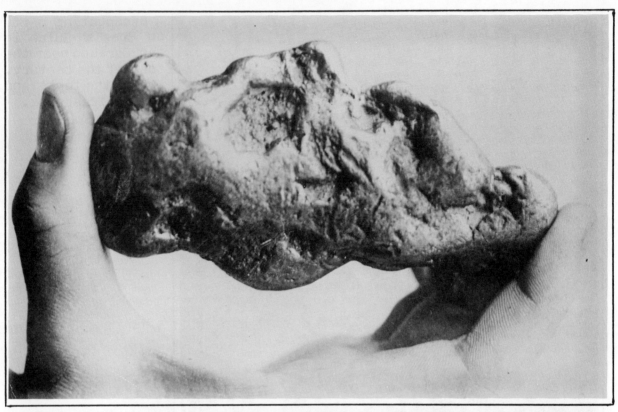

A gold nugget from the Cariboo. This is an actual size photograph of an
unusually large specimen of placer gold.   (Provincial Archives photo)

A few placer miners in front of Platt and Lyne's cabin on Cedar Creek
near the mouth of Quesnel Lake, 1921.

their supplies, but in the process their secret somehow slipped out. Some say a word which was carelessly dropped drew suspicion. Another version states that only their manner gave them away. In all the annals of placer mining seldom was the secret of a strike ever confined to the original discoverers. In any event by the time the two left Keithley Creek, scores of other miners on snowshoes and over several feet of snow, left with them. It was a winter stampede to new diggings and several days later the entire creek was heavily staked, the miners holding their ground by living in snow huts right on their claims.

But Antler Creek was only the gateway - beyond lay other creeks and unparalleled riches awaiting discovery. The next important discovery was made by a prospecting party which left Antler Creek and veered to the north-west. This party, including such individuals as the redoubtable Ned Stout, the trail-blazer Michael Byrnes, Vital Laforce, later of Omineca fame, William Dietz, Costello and Brown, explored the upper section of an unnamed creek and in a canyon found coarse colours in every pan. The best pan of the day ran $1.25 and was washed by William or "Dutch Bill" Dietz, and in honour of this accomplishment the party decided that the creek should be named after him, thus "Williams" Creek received its name. Strangely, fate frowned on most of the original discovery party, Dietz, his name perpetuated forever by one of the richest placer gold creeks in the world, staked one of the poorest sections on the entire stream and only 16 years later died in poverty and obscurity in Victoria, far from the scene of his epic find.

Although Williams Creek ultimately became the greatest placer gold creek in the province, it gave little indication at first that it would become such a fabulous producer. In those first months it was "spotty" in many places and the returns were often so poor that for a time it was known as "Humbug Creek." Most of the mining was initially confined to the ground above the canyon where the diggings were shallow with the "pay" being found from the surface down to a hard blue clay or hardpan. Later

The main street of Stanley about 1900.

this layer was penetrated to true bedrock, and there astonishing amounts of gold were found. It the start of a new era.

By 1861 the entire region was swarming with prospectors and as they spread out more new placer creeks came to light. Two of the most prominent of these were Lightning and Lowhee. Many of the streams received their names on the spot and these two were no exception. The former obtained its name through the use of an odd expression when Bill Cunningham, one of the discoverers of the creek, christened it.

When encountering anything difficult Cunningham was in the habit of referring to it as "lightning." The discovery trip proved particularly arduous and as the prospectors were slowly making their way along its steep banks they came to an almost impassable place. Cunningham is said to have paused, and after silently sizing up the situation for a few moments, finally exclaimed, "Boys, this is lightning." And it was.

Lowhee, on the other hand, picked up its unusual name in 1861 when its locator, Richard Willoughby, dubbed it "Lowhee" after a society of miners in Yale in which he had once played an important role.

After the deep mining began on the upper part of Williams Creek, the output of gold climbed. The Abbott and Jordan claim produced a minimum of 120 ounces per day; a correspondent of the day reported that they had a sack of gold fourteen inches high in their cabin. Another **claim**, the Steele, also above the canyon, was taking out an equivalent amount, and in one day recovered 33 pounds of gold.

"Toy," a Keithley Creek celebrity, standing in front of a cabin in the Chinese section of that old gold camp. 1896.

The miners of the Minnehaha Claim on Mosquito Creek pose for the camera in the late 1860s. Mosquito Creek, foot for foot, was the richest placer stream in British Columbia. Mined off and on for well over a century, it is considered by some mining men to have deep virgin ground even today. Strangely, it never achieved the fame it deserved.

A six-horse team hauling a massive key-stone drill through the town of Stanley around 1921. These drills were used to test the values of placer ground.

Elsewhere the results were equally as good. On Lowhee, Willoughby extracted over $50,000 in gold from his claim in a month and a half, and scores of others did as well on that productive creek. The returns from Lightning were also spectacular. In one historic three day span, a miner named Ned Campbell took out a total of 141 pounds of gold, 75 pounds of that in the first day of mining after striking pay.

While the stars of Williams, Lightning and Lowhee were rising, the fortunes of a few of the older creeks were declining. The returns from Antler Creek, while still good, were not in the same category as the former creeks, and Keithley, although still paying exceptionally well in places, was beginning to slip.

The output for 1861 was an official $2,666,118 and most of it was from the Cariboo, thus establishing it as the premier gold-field in the province. The most startling discovery, however, was yet to be made - the deep ground below the canyon on Williams Creek lay vacant, waiting to be tapped. This story, although related many times and in many ways, is still a compelling account.

In 1862, more strikes were made on new creeks like Van Winkle and Jack of Clubs and work continued on Lightning, Williams, Lowhee and the others. In the early summer of that year, however, Ned Stout, always in the forefront in prospecting, decided to try mining in a gulch below the canyon. Others had been there before him, had tested the ground and had found it disappointing and had moved on. Curious, Stout dug into the gravel until he hit the usual run of Williams Creek gold - well worn and dark yellow. Still not satisfied he sunk his shaft deeper and finally struck a second and much heavier run of gold - gold which was bright, angular and of greater purity than the usual Williams Creek gold. This

Some miners and their wives pose in front of the workings on Stout's Gulch in the Cariboo. Circa 1868.

was the first clue indicating that another and possibly richer paystreak was to be found below the canyon. Strangely, few were impressed by Stout's discovery, but one, an ex-sailor named William Barker, was convinced that Stout's find was not merely accidental but a harbinger of things to come.

Many legends shroud Barker today but one of the most persistent, and perhaps worthy of mention, is the story that Barker, soon after his arrival in the Cariboo was plagued by a recurring dream in which the number 52 kept reappearing. Whether this is fact or myth we will never know, but we do know that this illiterate miner formed a company in early August and staked a claim below the canyon - determined to test his theory. His enterprise was viewed with undisguised ridicule by nearly all the miners on the creek.

Ignoring the jibes, Barker's company erected a shaft-house and began inching their way through the rocks and gravel. Down they went; at 10 feet it was barren, again at 20 and 30. Even at 40 feet there was no sign of gold. At this point most miners would have abandoned the project, but prodded by Barker they continued. At 50 feet it was still barren. Then, just two feet deeper - at 52 feet, they struck it. A pan of dirt yielded $5 in coarse gold and a foot of ground produced an astounding $1,000. The word flashed along the creeks, "Billy Barker has struck the lead on Williams Creek on the flat below the canyon at a depth of fifty-two feet, obtaining $5 to the pan."

Several days later the Canadian Company struck astonishing pay in their shaft and a few days later "Cariboo Cameron" and his partners hit the lead farther down the creek.

Prospector Cliff Brown examining a tripping device used to regulate the flow of water from his dam to the workings on Little Hixon. 1971.

Barkerville, the metropolis of the goldfields, in 1868.

The almost legendary J. B. Hobson, owner of the celebrated Bullion Mine. This photograph was taken in 1902 and shows Hobson posing by a black bear he had just killed.

The scramble for ground below the canyon quickly turned into a mad rush. By late summer the creek was staked for a full seven miles and the area resounded with the sounds of miners at work, as company after company began sinking shafts to reach the paydirt.

By the end of 1862 the official output of gold from British Columbia was $2,656,903 and most of it had come from the rich deep diggings of Williams Creek.

The next year, 1863, was destined to become the most productive year for placer gold in the history of the province. Along Williams Creek the activity continued at a feverish pace. Below the canyon several fledgling camps appeared; one of them called "Barkerville" in honour of Billy Barker, and although there were several short-lived rival towns, this collection of shacks, log cabins and sundry businesses quickly established itself as the center of trade. With almost 4,000 miners working on Williams Creek alone, it was ideally situated. Along its saloon-lined main street the miners could be seen; quenching their thirst or trying their luck at the numerous games of chance.

In its heyday it was the most colourful placer gold camp in the province with a population verging on 6,000. And in 1863 it was quite a town. The harvest of gold from the creek seemed never-ending and some

An hydraulic elevator at Ward's Mine on the Horsefly River. This operation reputedly produced $1,000,000 in placer gold.

of the results were incredible.

Howay and Scholefield's "British Columbia" mentions the returns at some length and a few excerpts from that generally accurate source are indicative:

"The Diller took out 102 pounds Troy in a single day."

This was an unbelievable yield for one day's mining from a single claim. Diller, the major shareholder, swore that he wouldn't leave the Cariboo until he could match his weight in gold. It was quite a boast as he weighed almost 240 pounds, but when he left a few months later, he had not only taken out gold to equal his own weight but that of his dog and many more pounds besides.

Again Howay and Scholefield mention:

"The Cunningham produced, on an average, $2,000 per day during the whole season...."

"Forty claims at least paid handsomely, and from about twenty was taken out steadily, every twenty-four hours, from seventy to four hundred ounces."

Some miners cleaning the bedrock in Stout's Gulch. This is one of the most interesting jobs in placer mining.   (Archives photograph)

Poker chips from Madame Bendixon's Saloon in old Barkerville. Unusually rare, these items were made from ivory and hand engraved.

Quesnellemouth in 1899. This is the city of Quesnel today.

And so it went, all through 1863, and at the end of that year the official yield had skyrocketed to $3,913,563, although other contemporary accounts place the total at closer to $6,000,000.

Through the following two years the returns remained well above the $3,000,000 mark. Most of the gold by then was being produced by the deep workings. The surface diggings, although good in places, were largely depleted and new strikes, once so common, were less frequent.

By the early 1870s much of the interest had shifted northward with the discoveries of the Omineca and then the great Cassiar placers. In 1874, however, there were still 1,084 miners in the Cariboo district. The majority of them on Williams, Lightning and Grouse creeks. Farther to the south the Chinese, 120 in number, were mining along the Quesnel River close to old Quesnel Forks.

As the years passed, the output slowly declined and as the surface miners moved out the hydraulic outfits moved in. Where once the water-wheels had been king the monitors took their place. By the turn of the century only a few score die-hard miners remained where there had been thousands a few decades before. And when once the values in a cubic yard had been calculated in dollars, they were now calculated in cents, and the hydraulickers made money where the individual miner could never have made it pay. Some of the operations were gigantic, like Hobson's Bullion Mine near Likely and Ward's Mine on the Horsefly, but the romance was gone, the colourful mining days of the Cariboo were over.

Today there are still a few individual miners in that historic part of British Columbia, but most of those magnificent placer creeks of the past lie abandoned, their gravels worked and re-worked by generations of

The Output of Some of the Old Claims on Williams Creek in the Cariboo

No.	Name	Output
1.	Tiger	
2.	Beaver	
3.	Richfield	} Not bottomed
4.	John Bull	
5.	Columbia	$ 25,000
6.	Farmer	25,000
7.	Union	50,000
8.	Marysville	300,000
9.	Phelan	250,000
10.	Hart	250,000
11.	Oram	75,000
12.	Adams	300,000
13.	Elliott	100,000
14.	Bruce	100,000
15.	Rankin	75,000
16.	Prince of Wales	250,000
17.	Chee Chee	50,000
18.	Raby	500,000
19.	Dead Broke	150,000
20.	Prairie Flower	100,000
21.	Cameron	800,000
22.	Forest Rose	480,000
23.	California Tunnel	25,000
24.	Watty	300,000
25.	Tinker	300,000
26.	Moffatt	250,000
27.	Last Chance	150,000
28.	Beauregard	100,000
29.	Star	50,000
30.	McLean	50,000
31.	New York	50,000
32.	Grizzly	50,000
33.	Caledonia	750,000
34.	Never Sweat	250,000
35.	Nevada	25,000
36.	Morning Star	50,000
37.	Lillooett	100,000
37a		50,000
38.	Borealis	50,000
39.	Aurora	850,000
40.	Watson	150,000
41.	Davis	350,000
42.	Cariboo	300,000
43.	Pocohontas	125,000
44.	Walsh	75,000
45.	Wake-up Jake	175,000
46.	Australian	100,000
47.	Baldhead	350,000

No.	Name	Output
48.	Michaels	$ 50,000
49.	Saw Mill	150,000
50.	Ericson	500,000
51.	Hibernia	50,000
52.	Barker	600,000
53.	Sheepskin	150,000
54.	Eagle	10,000
55.	Sheepshead	25,000
56.	Loring	} 10,000
57.	"	
58.	Foster Campbell	125,000
59.	Canadian	350,000
60.	Diller	350,000
61.	Chips	75,000
62.	Black Jack and Burns Tunnel	} 675,000
63.	Discovery	50,000
64.	High Low Jack	50,000
65.	Pioneer	75,000
66.	Floyd	100,000
67.	Alturis	275,000
68.	Taff Vale	300,000
69.	Jenkins	175,000
70.	Mucho Oro	50,000
71.	Wyoming	50,000
72.	Cunningham	250,000
73.	Bell & Fulford	75,000
74.	San Francisco	50,000
75.	Adams	75,000
76.	Greer	125,000
77.	Abbott	150,000
78.	Tontine	50,000
79.	12 Foot Davis	15,000
80.	Little Diller	25,000
81.	Point	100,000
82.	Steele	600,000
83.	Tyack	75,000
84.	Six-Toed Pete	50,000
85.	Cornish	} 200,000
86.	French	
87.	Browse	100,000
88.	Steadman	50,000
89.	Dutch Bill	200,000
90.	Red Jacket	25,000
91.	Scott	25,000
92.	Wilson	200,000
93.	Wheal Mary Ann	100,000
94.	Casket	50,000

miners. Occasionally they come across pay which was missed by the white and Chinese argonauts so long ago, those are the times when visions of another Cedar Creek flicker ever so briefly before their eyes, and all the lonely hours of prospecting seem worthwhile.

THE PLACER CREEKS

Any attempt to analyze the possibilities of the placer creeks of the Cariboo is not only impossible but also presumptuous. There are experienced miners who have spent their entire lives on one stream and have still failed to solve its many riddles.

This section, therefore, will be devoted to a short survey of a few of the major creeks. A substantial list of other placer gold streams in the Cariboo will also be included.

It should also be mentioned that on certain creeks, like parts of Williams Creek, miners are not allowed to work. Because of its historic significance it has been protected by law and mining of any kind is prohibited. There are other old placer streams which also fall into this category, both in the Cariboo and elsewhere in the province.

<u>Antler Creek</u> - Discovered in the fall of 1860 by trail-blazer John Rose and his partners. By the summer of 1861 this amazing stream was producing $10,000 per day and some of the ground surrendered an incredible $1,000 per square foot of bedrock. The Sawmill Flat area was considered the richest section, the canyons the poorest.

A waterwheel on Chisholm Creek in 1868.

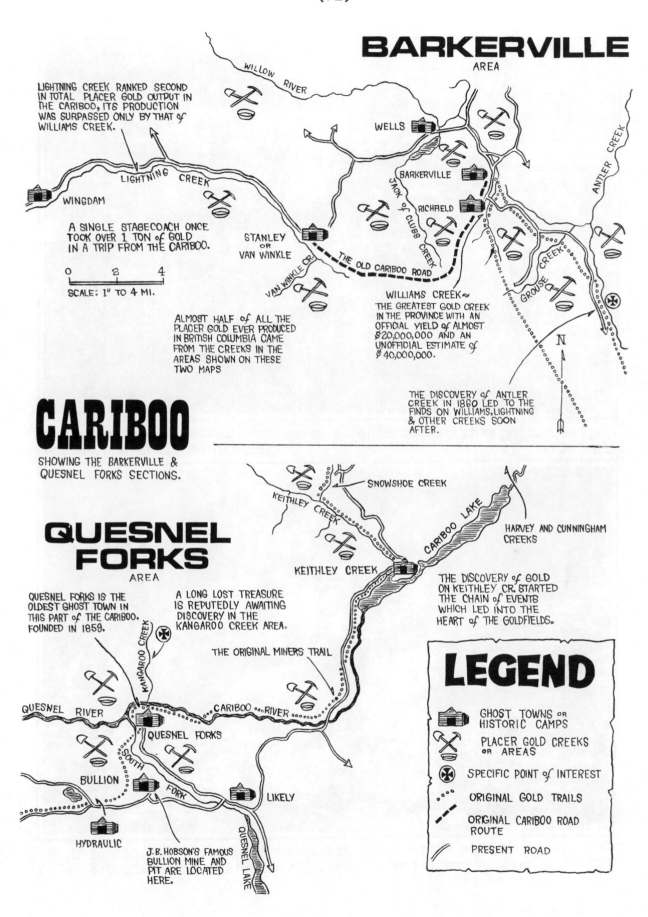

A prospecting outfit preparing to cross the Quesnel River on a ferry in 1913.   (Bureau of Mines photograph)

Two Japanese and a white miner preparing to blast a boulder at J. B. Hobson's Bullion operation in 1897. (Provincial Archives photograph)

This historic creek has been drifted, hydraulicked, ground sluiced and hand mined for years by a number of experienced miners.

The possibility of buried channels still exists although the old-timers sunk shafts, unsuccessfully, in attempts to tap buried channels.

On upper Antler Creek the rich pay-streak started near the mouth of Victoria Creek, the diggings above being much leaner than below. The gold was generally coarse and nuggety in character.

Still an interesting creek despite decades of mining.

Cunningham Creek - Discovered in 1861 by William Cunningham, one of the most successful miners ever in Cariboo. One crevice on the "Discovery" claim yielded 600 ounces of gold. Abandoned after 1861 in 1864 a group of four men found rich diggings on bedrock only about eight to ten feet below the surface and quietly took out 100 ounces per day until their discovery became known and the creek was stampeded. Generally the gold from this creek is not as coarse as other creeks in the region and is, with few exceptions, known as "flaxseed" gold.

The richest section of Cunningham Creek was from the old Discovery Claim to Palmer's old hydraulic mine, The narrow, rich pay-streak was on the upper part of the creek.

Miners like McGregor, Thompson, Ross, Tregillus and many others, including the Chinese, worked this creek for years.

Dragon Creek - Discovered in the early 1860s by a Frenchman, nicknamed "The Dragon" because of his fighting abilities, the creek was so named.

The gold from Dragon Creek was coarse, nuggety and assayed as high

VAN WINKLE. (1927) LONGSTAFF 1437

The deserted main street of Stanley as it looked in 1927.

as .950 fine. Like most of the other placer streams in the area it has been drifted, sluiced, hydraulicked and drilled. The gold is local in origin and occurs mostly on or very close to bedrock.

Fine miners like "One-eyed" Davis, the Hauser brothers, Muller and scores of others mined this creek for years.

Grouse Creek - Discovered to be gold-bearing in 1861 it was mined that season sporadically and then abandoned. In 1864 it came to prominence again when the Heron Company discovered a lost channel. The Heron Claim ultimately produced over $400,000 (over $7 millions at today's rates), and established the creek as a major producer.

The gold from Grouse Creek was heavy and nuggety. Numerous mining companies worked this creek; the Full Rig, Black Hawk, Canadian, Heron and dozens of others and miners like Allen, Jarvis and Pomeroy spent a long time attempting to solve its riddles.

Worked heavily in the mid-1860s and the 1870s, it has been mined by all the conventional methods.

Jack of Clubs Creek - Discovered in 1861 this creek, although considered potentially great, never came up to expectations. It did produce about $400,000 to $450,000 in gold in the early years. The gold was sometimes coarse and ran about .850 in purity.

Although the "pay" on this stream tends to be "patchy" and it has been mined for well over a century, there are still some definite possibilities. There are experienced miners in the region who still contend that the high channel on the north-east side of the creek has yet to be exploited.

Lightning Cr.
Point Claim, Cariboo, - 194¼ Ounces Clean Gold
for 2 days Work 1902

194¼ ounces of coarse gold and nuggets from the famous Point Claim in 1902. Worth nearly $58,000 today, it was the result of only two days work then.

Some placer miners posing in front of the Aurora Claim on Williams Creek in 1867. This claim held the distinction of producing the highest official yield of gold of any placer mine in the Cariboo, a total of $850,000. But the true total was probably much higher as most of the companies, for varying reasons, declared considerably less than the actual yield.

Gold from Cedar Creek in 1921. More than $10,000 in raw gold value is represented in the three pans. At today's prices the gold would be worth more than $150,000.   (Provincial Archives photograph)

Keithley Creek - This placer creek flows into Cariboo Lake from the west.
Discovered in 1860 by "Doc" Keithley, after whom it was named. Over the
years it has produced prodigious amounts of gold, much of it coarse and
nuggety. Two tributaries, French Snowshoe and Little Snowshoe, flowing
into Keithley from the north, have also been prominent producers.

This creek was hand mined extensively and later hydraulicked by a
number of companies many of whom did exceptionally well. A tough creek
to work, there are still areas which have interesting possibilities.

Lightning Creek - Found early in 1861 William Cunningham, Bell and Hume
this creek flows into the Swift River. It ultimately yielded more gold
than any other creek in Cariboo except Williams Creek.

The gold from this creek was unusually coarse and nuggety with the
largest nugget in the Cariboo, a 30 ounce 1 pennyweight piece, found on
Butcher Bench in 1864. This creek has numerous gold-bearing branches;
Amador Creek, Perkins Creek, Grub Gulch, Van Winkle Creek, Davis Creek,
Anderson Creek, Last Chance Creek, Jawbone Creek and several others. A
noted characteristic, and difficulty, of Lightning Creek was the depth
of the bedrock and the subsequent flooding of the deep diggings. In the
season of 1876 half a dozen companies were operating pumps twenty-four
hours a day and raising almost 20 million gallons per day in an effort
to keep the ground drained.

There have been various estimates concerning the total production
from Lightning Creek. Although the official yield is somewhat lower, a
figure of $12,000,000 to $15,000,000 is probably fairly accurate. Edw.
Campbell, in 1861, recovered an astonishing 1,700 ounces in only three
days washing. The number of companies who profitably mined this stream

A view of Quesnel Forks showing the town as it appeared in the late
1880s when the camp was on the decline.

is impressive. An interesting feature of Lightning Creek is that the tributaries of the creek on the south side were rich in gold but those on the north side contained little gold.

Many experienced Cariboo miners contend that the gravels of this stream still hold more gold than any other placer creek in the Cariboo, and they may be correct.

A few miners, like Tom Crawford, continue to work leases on this historic creek, and are doing relatively well.

One of the most fascinating creeks in Cariboo.

Lowhee Creek - Discovered in 1861 by Richard Willoughby this creek was amazingly productive in the 1860s. The richest ground was near where the stream flows into the meadows.

The gold was coarse and nuggety. Miners like John Hopp worked it for years with considerable success. A clean-up as late as 1915 yielded 2,300 ounces (about $690,000 at today's prices). This famous creek has been sluiced, drifted, hydraulicked and generally mined by every possible method. Lowhee has been well worked.

Mosquito Creek - Discovered to be gold-bearing in 1861 this particular creek holds the distinction of being richer, foot for foot, than any other placer stream in the province, including both the better known Williams and Lightning creeks. It produced an estimated $3,500,000 in gold at $17 an ounce (at today's rates an astonishing $63 millions in gold) out of only about 1,500 running feet of ground.

A tributary of the Willow River the richest ground was the gulch of Mosquito Creek, about 1000 feet from the Willow River. A tributary called Red Gulch was not nearly as rich. Mosquito has, over the years, been extensively drifted and later hydraulicked. A few Cariboo miners contend that there is still ground worth working along this creek.

Interesting ground.

Williams Creek - Discovered in 1861 by a party composed of "Dutch Bill" Dietz, Stout, Vital, Byrnes, Brown, Costello and possibly several more prospectors. This creek was the most renowned gold creek in the entire province and one of the most famous in the west. A semi-official yield of $20,000,000 and other estimates range up to $40,000,000 the actual production probably lies somewhere in between those two figures.

There were two major runs of gold on this creek, the first was on shallow ground above the canyon, the second, which made the reputation of the creek and of the Cariboo, was found below the canyon. The credit for the discovery of the second run, which was astoundingly rich, went to Billy Barker although it probably should have gone to Ned Stout who made the initial discovery in Stouts Gulch. His find led to the later discoveries by Barker, "Cariboo Cameron" and others who are far better known. Williams Creek has been exposed to practically every known mode of mining. The early rockers, sluices, shafts and drifts later gave way to hydraulicking.

This celebrated creek has been worked and re-worked so many times that it defies belief. Protected in most areas by provincial government legislation, it is still regarded as the great El dorado placer creek of British Columbia, a reputation justly earned.

CONCLUSION

The gold trails which reverberated to the footsteps of thousands of miners more than a century ago lie overgrown and neglected. Most of the once booming camps of the past have disappeared or lie in ruins. Barkerville still stands, a far different town than it once was, but there are places where little has changed, where the Cariboo of more than a hundred years ago doesn't seem too far away. Places like Little Snowshoe Creek, Quesnel Forks, Last Chance Creek, Harvey Creek and a handful of other spots have somehow retained the mood of the discovery years.

The vastness of the Cariboo hasn't changed much and the region is still studded with gold creeks. Streams which once yielded more than $50,000,000 in gold flow on although much of the easy ground has been mined extensively a persevering prospector can still recover some of that intriguing metal and something more besides - the delicate mood of a vanished era. This is the place for those who like to wander on past the outposts of civilization.

Stand along on the deserted streets of old Quesnel Forks when the half-light of a dying day is slowly moving across the waters of that river called the Quesnel - then you're in the Cariboo.

The cemetery at Stanley today, the old burying ground of many Cariboo miners in the early years.

XI

FRASER RIVER

The most amazing road-building feat in the old West, the Cariboo
Road. This was the view at 17 Mile Bluff near Spuzzum.

INTRODUCTION

Fraser River - It began on the Fraser in 1858.

There are countless versions concerning the events which ultimately led to the "Fraser River Excitement." The name of the individual who was responsible for triggering the great stampede to the river may never be known, for placer gold was discovered in several places in British Columbia prior to 1858.

One of the earliest records states that the Thompson River Indians made the initial discovery either on the Tranquille River or on the main Thompson near the mouth of the Nicoamen River in 1852. Chief Trader Roderick McLean at Fort Kamloops, a notorious character in many respects, did purchase some gold on behalf of the Hudson's Bay Company and had amassed, by 1856, "two pint pickle bottles half full of gold."

Another version, substantiated by several letters of 1856 states that gold was found at both Thompson's River and at Fort Hope. There is also evidence that another "strike" was made in 1857 at "The Forks," that is, the confluence of the great Fraser and the beautiful Thompson, close to where historic old Lytton now stands. This find was supposedly made by American miners who had drifted into that region by way of the Okanagan.

By 1857, a year before the great rush started, it was common local

A prospector panning for gold in British Columbia.

A British Columbia Express Co. stagecoach on the Cariboo Road. Known as the "B.X." this company was the greatest stagecoach line in the history of the Canadian west, even surpassing in some respects its more famous American counterparts like Wells, Fargo & Company and the equally well known Butterfield Overland Express. It ran for more than fifty years along that renowned road and carried most of the gold from the Cariboo during that span, losing only two shipments to highwaymen.

This was Lytton's original "lock-up" as it appeared in 1921. Most of the towns along the Fraser River in the early years had log jails for the imprisonment of lawbreakers.

(102)

knowledge that in the "Couteau Country," as the vast area east of Lytton was then called, placer gold in increasing quantities was being found.

That careful historian, Captain John T. Walbran, in his work, "British Columbia Coast Names," stated that the first news of gold on the Fraser was carried south to San Francisco by the crew of the U.S.S. Active, a survey ship which, in late 1857, was engaged in fixing the position of the 49th parallel, and while so employed was asked by the officers of H. M. S. Plumper, to convey a prisoner named Macaulay to Esquimalt. While the culprit was being transported he displayed to the crew of the ship a large poke full of gold-dust which, he stated, he had procured in trade from the Fraser River Indians. This disclosure evidently caused a considerable stir on board the American vessel.

When the Active returned to San Francisco that winter, the news of a new gold field on a river in British Territory, beyond the 49th parallel, soon made the rounds of the port city. Interest was further fanned when the Hudson's Bay Company, in February of 1858, sent an 800 ounce shipment of gold-dust, in charge of a Mr. Holt, to the United States Mint in that city. That was proof enough - by March the first bands of American argonauts were on the Fraser and were immediately rewarded by the discovery of an astoundingly rich bar just below Fort Yale. The bar was "Hill's Bar."

By April, hundreds of miners were on their way north and they were

Yale, the metropolis of the gold-fields in 1858. Boasting a population of more than 3,000 miners at its height, this town was the center of mining activity on the Fraser River in the early years.

soon to be followed by thousands more. The rush had begun.

Victoria was inundated by hordes of miners and adventurers as ships like the Commodore, Pacific, Santa Cruz and dozens of others deposited their human cargo. In a single day, July 8th, 1858, a total of 2,800 people arrived in Victoria. In that hectic first year it has been estimated that no less than 23,000 people set out for the new Eldorado by both land and sea. Considering the conditions at the time, a surprisingly high percentage of them actually made it to the Fraser River.

It was found that the lower reaches of the river were barren of gold but just above Fort Langley the gold began to show. Fargo's Bar was the first to produce and was followed by myriads of others, some with colourful names like Murderer's, Poverty, Yankee Doodle, Eagle, Texas, Trinity and Cisco. In that year gold-bearing bars were found all the way from Fort Langley as far up as Pavillion, a distance of nearly two hundred miles, and there were miners strung out all along the river between these two points.

The returns varied widely, with some of the poorer bars paying only $5 or $6 per day, while on some of the richer bars like Hill's, Mormon, Boston and others the yield was excellent. It was acknowledged by all that the richest of all the bars on the Fraser was Hill's Bar, situated about 1½ miles below Yale. Its paystreak was fully half a mile long, sixty feet wide and over five feet deep and from it a total of well over $1,000,000 was taken. In Howay and Scholefield's "British Columbia," several extracts serve to indicate its early riches:

Some Indians working a bar with rockers near the confluence of the Fraser and the Thompson rivers.

Front Street in Yale in 1882 with the sternwheeler "R. P. Rithet" tied up at Steamboat Landing.

A scow running the Grand Canyon of the Fraser in the early days.

Lytton in the early 1860's. The gold seekers had gone on to Cariboo and the old town, once a booming mining camp, lapsed into obscurity.

Courtesy of the B. C. Provincial Museum, Victoria, B. C.

"At Hill's Bar...a man, with four assistants, was taking out $400 a day."

And again:

"....it is recorded that Mr. Winston and two partners took out forty-six pounds of gold dust between December, 1858, and April, 1859. Frequently they obtained fifty ounces in a day and sometimes, when the sluices were running day and night, seventy to eighty ounces in the same time."

Although most of the miners were working the bars, there were a few places where bench diggings were remunerative. The dry diggings near the Fountain gave spectacular results in 1858. The average yield of five rockers for one week was $47.09 per day each.

The year ended with a recorded $520,353.00 in placer gold returns although the actual take was probably much higher as many miners never disclosed their results.

The total number of miners on the Fraser in 1858 was approximately 10,000 and there were others on the Thompson. Most of the miners were Americans and there were, like most other frontier areas in the west, a number of renegades and ne'er-do-wells amongst them.

The only law on the river in the early part of 1858 was "Miners' Law" and it soon became evident that this type of law was inadequate.

There were several occurrences in that year which pointed to the necessity of establishing a permanent civil service - including law enforcement officers.

The first indications of serious trouble became apparent in early August when the scalped bodies of several miners were found floating down the Fraser. This was the initial phase of the "Fraser River Indian War," a short but bloody affray in which a score of prospectors and an equal number of Indians were to lose their lives. This clash between the Indians, led by the formidable Thompson River chief, Spitlum, and the miners, was caused primarily by the high-handed treatment of the Indians by the whites.

By the middle of August most of the miners who had been mining north of Yale were back in that center, having been forced to withdraw from their up-river "diggings" by hostile Indians. A punitive expedition under a "Captain" Rouse, was sent against the Indians and inflicted serious casualties upon them. Unfortunately, most of the bands punished were innocent.

As the month progressed the Indian war grew more intense and a mass meeting, attended by more than 2,000 miners, was called in Yale to bring the troubles to an end. A call for volunteers resulted in the formation of two separate companies of miners. The larger force under the command of "Captain" Snyder, succeeded in forcing their way up the Big Canyon and at China Bar they arrived just in time to rescue five miners who had been holding off a superior force of Indians from behind an earthworks fortification. Every one of the men, the last survivors of an original group which had numbered twenty-six, was wounded, and one, a prospector named Edward Stout, had been wounded no less than seven times. Stout, however, soon recovered and joined the vanguard into the Cariboo soon after, where Stout's Gulch still commemorates

A W. S. Hatton painting of "A scene at the Fountain near Parsonville, Fraser River." This watercolour was executed in 1864.

A gold dredge working at Boston Bar in 1897.

Some Canadian, Chinese and American coins and tokens recovered from the streets of old Yale.

his name. Little affected by his injuries he finally died at old Yale at the venerable age of 99.

The second company of volunteers under "Captain" Graham was less fortunate as both Graham and his second-in-command were shot and killed by Indians at Long Bar for having trampled on a flag of truce.

An uneasy armistice between the prospectors and the Indians was established shortly after the last expedition. The news of the war, however, reached Governor Douglas in Victoria and by the end of August he was in Yale where he quickly set up a civil service and appointed peace officers.

Gunplay was frequent all through 1858 and there were many cases of deaths by shooting.

On Douglas' trip he was forced to appoint a drumhead jury to try a certain William King for the murder of a miner named Eaton, who had been shot to death by the former at Cross Bar, at the foot of the Big Canyon.

The Correspondence between Richard Hicks, an official at Yale, and Governor Douglas, further confirms the claim that there was little law and order along the river in that year.

On October 17, 1858, Hicks wrote:

"Issac C. Miller was fatally wounded by Henry Post. The trouble arose over the right to a claim at Madison Bar above Yale...."

An early view of the Colonial Hotel at once-thriving Soda Creek.

But these occurrences, serious as they were, were of little concern to the main body of miners, for they had noticed, as they ascended the river, that the gold became coarser. Thus, a theory became accepted - somewhere, on or beyond the upper reaches of the Fraser, awaited the almost legendary "motherlode," the origin of the placer gold.

With the low water in the early spring of 1859, the ascent of the river began. Thousands of argonauts left Yale by boat and trail and more poured northward over the newly constructed route from Douglas to Lillooet. Whereas in 1858 the main mining activity had been from Yale south, in 1859, it was north of Lytton.

As the prospectors proceeded up-river, rich bars and dry diggings were encountered all along the way. By May, the Quesnel River, an eastern tributary of the Fraser, had been reached. At the junction some of the vanguard pressed on, but others, drawn by the lure of a new watercourse, branched eastward on the Quesnel. The bars of the tributary proved rich, and, unknown to the miners, they were fast approaching their goal. They were balanced on the threshold of the renowned "Cariboo."

The following year the first strikes were made in the Cariboo and it was soon to become the premier gold-field of British Columbia, far surpassing any before it and any after. And the Fraser, the mainstay of the miners for two years, was suddenly dwarfed by this new Eldorado.

But the story of the Cariboo is a separate story in itself, and although the Fraser was relegated to a lesser role, its gold-bearing gravels were far from depleted.

Lillooet in 1864. This watercolour by atrist W. S. Hatton shows the town as it looked in the years when the Cariboo was at its height and Lillooet was one of the gateways to the gold-fields. The Fraser River was also producing considerable quantities of gold at this time.

   Although many miners abandoned the Fraser in favour of Cariboo,
others stayed on, working and re-working its bars and prospecting for
new "diggings."
   Hill's Bar continued to pay and so did some of the other larger
bars. New operations were commenced on dry diggings on all sections
of the river and some rewarding results were obtained.
   Some of the other rivers emptying into the Fraser were looked at
more thoroughly, with the Bridge River near Lillooet and some of its
tributaries proving especially good. A considerable amount of placer
gold being obtained from its mouth up to the head of "Deep Canyon."
Coarse gold was also found farther up the Bridge with both the South
Fork and Cadwallader Creek giving good returns.
   Mr. A. W. Smith, the Government Agent at Lillooet, in his report
of Sept. 27th, 1876, stated:

"All the mining in this portion of the district is carried
  on by Chinese and Indians and is confined to the banks of
  the Fraser and Bridge Rivers. The Chinese are mostly engaged
  on the Fraser and use sluice boxes where water can be got,
  the rocker is also used, especially early and late in the
  season, when the water is low, and very rich deposits are
  often found. In some localities the gold is coarse while
  in others it is very fine and quicksilver has to be used
  to save it. The mining season is about eight months, from
  the middle of March to the middle of November.
     There are about three hundred Indians who mine more or
  less during the season; they prefer the Bridge River and
  the localities on the Fraser where the gold is coarse; they
  use the rocker and save the gold by means of a blanket or
  gunny sack in the bottom of the rocker; they often find
  rich spots among the rocks where neither whites nor Chinese

Two Chinese miners rocking for gold in the Fraser Canyon in the 1890s.

look for gold. Last spring, in March, one family of Indians,
about 10 miles below Lillooet on the Fraser River, took
$1,500 from a crevice of a rock."

And the silent Chinese, always reluctant to leave a sure thing,
continued to sluice and rock all along the river, often re-working
ground which had already been mined, and obtaining sometimes excellent
returns. The river grudgingly yielded her gold but the quantity, once
so spectacular, was diminishing steadily.

Occasionally, however, new pockets and sometimes even new creeks
were discovered. The most notable example of the latter occurred in
the spring of 1886, when a party of Chinese prospectors discovered
coarse gold and nuggets on Cayoosh Creek about 6 miles from Lillooet.
It was an incredible find for this creek had been bypassed for nearly
three decades by thousands of white miners until the Chinese finally
found it.

By the turn of the century the production had declined to the
point where even the Chinese miners were pulling out. The die had been
irrevocably cast by then, for when these inscrutable miners, endowed
with endless patience, gave up on an area - it was considered mined
out.

Today, there are still a few snipers at work along the river.
The yield is a mere fraction of its once prodigious returns, and the
once historic bars lie virtually undisturbed. And the river, which,
more than a hundred years ago, drew thousands of eager-eyed argonauts
to its gold-bearing gravels, flows on undisturbed.

The town of Douglas on the old Douglas-Lillooet Road in 1864.

THE PLACER CREEKS

The Fraser River is unlike any other placer gold region in British Columbia in that almost all of the total production of gold came from the main river and a few noted tributaries like the Coquihalla, Bridge and Lillooet rivers, and Siwash and Cayoosh creeks. The bars along the Fraser, however, probably contributed over 90% of the total amassed by the region.

There were 94 prominent bars, flats and riffles on the Fraser River between Sumas and a point about 30 miles above Lillooet which were noted placer gold producers in the early years. They stretched right from a bar called Fargo's, just above Sumas Village, up to Dancing Bill's Bar, some miles north of Lillooet. A number of the bars became famous in the late 1850's, the most celebrated being Hill's Bar, just below Yale. In a century its output has been calculated at $1,000,000. Other bars like Emory, Boston, Upper Mormon and Sailor also gained envious reputations for their production of gold.

Although the gold recovered on the bars and flats of the river was invariably fine grained, there were places where deposits of coarse or heavy gold was recovered. The Hill's Bar gold was significantly coarser than the gold found on the bars downriver from it. Heavy gold was also found on a stretch running from Boston Bar to Cisco Flat, located just below the town of Lytton. Another section which yielded heavy gold was from a point about half-way between Lytton and Lillooet and on upriver past Lillooet to the Fountain. Nuggets weighing as much as 6 ounces and many between 2 and 4 ounces were found in the Lillooet region.

The river was so productive that by the mid 1890's, there were 400 Chinese miners still gleaning its bars. Even today a few snipers still work some of the better bars every season in low water.

CONCLUSION

The canyon country of this river, especially between old Yale and Lillooet, is magnificent. Most of the bars have been mined extensively and their once-heralded output is exhausted but the scenery is beyond compare.

The Fraser is one of the last of the great rivers of the west which is still unspoiled and those stopping-places of a century ago, like old Lytton, Lillooet and Yale, have retained a touch of their charm.

This is matchless country - and you won't forget it.

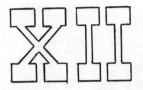

THOMPSON

INTRODUCTION

Thompson - As previously related, placer gold was discovered in this region before any other area in the province, including even the more celebrated Fraser River. From the finds in this area, the great rushes to the Fraser came about.

The initial discovery by Thompson River Indians, probably occurred as early as 1852, either on the Tranquille River near old Fort Kamloops, or near the mouth of the Nicoamen River which is a tributary of the main Thompson and lies between Lytton and Spences Bridge. The earliest activity was centered on or near the mouth of the Nicoamen.

Inevitably, however, white prospectors, hearing of the find, moved in and soon began to prospect further afield and the result was, by 1858, the epic stampede to the bars of the Fraser River.

In those first years the Thompson country, eclipsed by the gold recovered on the Fraser and later by the discovery of the much heralded Cariboo field, was neglected by all but a few miners. There was some mining on the main Thompson and at other places such as the Tranquille River but it was insignificant in comparison to the other regions.

With the passing of the first decade, however, and the depletion of the shallow diggings in the Cariboo, some prospectors returned to the Thompson River country, ever hopeful of finding new Eldorados.

In the next few decades they re-worked parts of the Thompson as miners like the Mahon brothers mined in localities like Horseshoe Bend, an old placer area below Deadman's Creek, others worked near the mouth of the Nicoamen and on the benches and bars elsewhere along that most unforgettable river.

In the Kamloops area the historic Tranquille was still yielding coarse gold and nuggets. Like miners everywhere, they were not content with known placer regions and were constantly on the lookout for new creeks. Louis Creek, a tributary of the North Thompson, first found in 1861, but given only a cursory examination then, was mined again more thoroughly. And other tributaries of the North Thompson were brought

The Nicoamen River emptying into the Thompson River. In the early 1850s, coarse placer gold was found close to the mouth of this river by an unknown Indian. The great rush to the Fraser and Thompson rivers started soon after the discovery.

into production and some of the bars of that river were found to carry gold.

Farther to the east, as the search widened, a new gold-bearing stream called "Scotch" was discovered by 1864. The gold in this creek was coarse and found in shallow ground, resulting in a small stampede to the area. For almost a decade a significant number of miners, both Chinese and white, obtained a respectable quantity of gold before it played out.

Although the Thompson country was auriferous in certain sections, the placer gold yield was never exciting, except in occasional areas like the Tranquille River and Scotch Creek, nor did their placers have the longevity of those of the Cariboo, Atlin or East Kootenay and by the turn of the century, most of the miners had moved on and activity had died down.

Today, those old areas still lie dormant and most of their gravels depleted of the treasure they once held. From time to time, however, a reminder of those years turns up; a tarnished Chinese coin, a rusty pick-head or an old and worn gold pan, but they are only the solitary mementoes of those days, for in most places where the miners toiled there is little evidence of their passing; sagebrush and sand have healed the scars.

THE PLACER CREEKS

● <u>North Thompson River</u> - The bars and benches of this river have yielded fine placer gold for years, especially in the section from Heffley Creek to Barriere. This river joins the South Thompson at Kamloops where the main Thompson is born. A number of tributaries of this river also carry gold, the most noted of which is Louis Creek which joins the river from the eastern side between Exlou and Barriere, other branches like Dixon and Jamieson creeks are also gold-bearing although the gold is inclined to be fine.

Prospects: This is not generally considered to be a good placer river although fine gold may be recovered in many places from Kamloops to Barriere. Some of the tributaries have possibilities.

● <u>Scotch Creek</u> - Probably found prior to 1864 by miners testing the creeks flowing into Shuswap Lake. This placer stream empties into that lake from the north side between Celista and the Adams Riber. The total production from this creek is estimated at around $50,000. The paying section is located about 7 or 8 miles from its mouth. In December of 1886, Mr. William Dodd, the Government Agent at Kamloops, reported:

"....Scotch Creek, falling into Shuswap Lake...is steep and contains large rocks which make the working expensive. The supply of water is abundant. The gold is bright and heavy and sells for $17 an ounce here. My estimate of $22,000 as the yield of this creek during the past season may be taken as approximately correct."

This creek was hand mined by whites and Chinese with rockers and sluices. The gold was quite coarse in most instances.

Prospects: Interesting. Some possibilities still exist although the "pay" section was limited.

● <u>Tranquille (Creek) River</u> - Discovered as early as 1852 and may have been the first stream in British Columbia to produce placer gold in quantity. Some historians claim that the discovery of gold on this river inaugurated the great stampede of prospectors into the province; eventually leading to the discovery of the Cariboo and other goldfields in British Columbia. Others state that this honour rightly belongs to the Nicoamen River and not to the Tranquille. The total output of gold from this river has been estimated at $250,000 and well may have reached that figure as it was mined steadily for more than half a century, first by whites and latterly by Chinese. This river is situated on the north side of Kamloops Lake almost 8 miles west of Kamloops.

Over a quarter of a century after the river had been discovered it was still being actively mined. In 1888, Frederick Hussey, the Government Agent at Kamloops, wrote:

"The mines on Tranquille Creek continue to yield a regular supply of coarse gold of first class quality, but as the

Nicola Indians near the turn of the century.

The "Big Bluff" on the Cariboo Road with the Thompson below.

claims are...controlled by Chinese, it is impossible to secure reliable information regarding the quantity of gold obtained. Between 30 and 40 Chinese are regularly employed in placer mining on this creek...."

Surprisingly, nuggets of the 1 ounce size were not unusual on this river and as a rule the gold was much coarser than that found on the North Thompson and its tributaries. It was worked extensively by practically every method of mining.

Prospects: An interesting river but it has been mined rather extensively so that there are only a few isolated places remaining which still warrant investigation today. Sniping in a few selected locations returns some gold.

A fully loaded stagecoach prepares to leave Ashcroft in the 1890s.

CONCLUSION

Step back a hundred years in this part of British Columbia, to the main Thompson, a river almost unchanged and indescribably beautiful, or up to the North Thompson valley, or east into the Shuswap.

Gold, that old lure, is gone, and in those places where the sound of miners at work once resounded along the rivers, a silence dominates the area. You may not recover much placer gold but you'll remember the sagebrush covered hills of the Thompson - the images of this part of the province are not easily forgotten.

XII

BIG BEND

Mining camp poker chips from the interior of British Columbia.

INTRODUCTION

Big Bend - Late in 1864, some miners from the Wild Horse region in the East Kootenay, hearing vague rumours of placer gold being found on the upper reaches of the Columbia River, headed north into that wild territory.

And on the bars of the river they found their gold, and although the yield varied from as little as 10 cents in some places, to as much as half a dollar to the pan in others, the word soon went out that it was as rich as Cariboo.

News of a strike has a strange way of spreading and by the early spring of 1865 hundreds of prospectors were in the locality. The cross section of miners was amazing; there were Americans in their fringed buckskins, French-Canadians and English Canadians and the ever present Chinese, all babbling with excitement. And as spring lengthened they continued to stream in; from the Fraser, Thompson and Shuswap in the west and from the Wild Horse and across the line in the south.

Virtually every miner there was confident that they were in on a strike which would equal, if not surpass, Cariboo. An old Fraser hand who was known as "Old Texas," exemplified the feelings of the miners at the new diggings when he stated:

"I would not take $10,000 and leave my claim unprospected; and all I have in the world is a sack of flour and five pounds of bacon and a cayuse in Colville."

By summer the pack trains of outfits like Smith and Lander and Romano were coming in over country which, in some places, was not even broken by well defined trails.

And on the creeks like French and McCulloch, Gold and Carnes, the miners had penetrated the gravels to bed-rock. The yield was not high, except in isolated spots, but the notion persisted that it was just temporary - that much richer ground would be discovered. And so it went, on through the summer, with the miners doggedly staying with the creeks, even when supplies ran so low at one point that they were forced to subsist on a diet which consisted, in miners' jargon, solely of "flour straight."

The yield that year was a disappointing $40,000, the bulk of which was obtained from French Creek, and the remainder from McCulloch and Carnes.

Despite the poor returns for the season, in 1866 hundreds more eager-eyed argonauts made their way into the new diggings - some coming in from the west over Moberly's newly widened trail, others coming up the Columbia from Colville and facing all to get to the gold-fields, even to challenging the dangerous "Death Rapids" or "Dalles des Morts," and losing sometimes. In one remembered catastrophe, 17 out of a total of 23 men perished when their boat overturned in an ill-fated attempt to run the rapids. But on they came, risking everything to reach the highly touted "shallow diggings" of the Big Bend.

In that year a few companies like The Guild and The Ridge made up to $3,000 each week and some individuals did equally as well, but the vast majority of the miners made little more than wages, and some not even enough to exist on. And although the yield climbed to $250,000 for the year; with $100,000 coming from each of the two main creeks, French and McCulloch, the end had come - the illusion was gone and the "Big Bend" became the "Big Bilk."

By the early fall of 1866 the gradual abandonement of the area had turned into a mass exodus. The shallow ground, once considered so rich, had been far below expectations and the auriferous gravels which still lay deep below the surface had yet to be tapped, for it was guarded in most places by huge boulders and underground streams which had baffled the attempts of most of the miners. The "poor man's diggings" had been found wanting and the deep diggings required both capital and equipment, neither of which the ordinary miner possessed. By 1874, the Big Bend was all but deserted.

In later years renewed attempts were made to work the placers and through the latter half of the 1880's and most of the 1890's, outfits like the Consolation and Glover companies experienced some success as did a few individual miners who had struck good "pay."

The efforts continued spasmodically for years and although most of the operations failed, a percentage succeeded. A century after the first prospectors had struck gold in the region, the total won from the gravels of the Big Bend stood at a respectable $2,000,000. Much of it in coarse gold and nuggets.

Today, the hydro projects in the area have dampened the enthusiasm of the prospectors who still feel that it has only relinquished a part of its hoard. But there are still individuals who continue to work its gravels, especially along French and McCulloch creeks, searching for a new lead or an unworked deposit of "pay."

THE PLACER CREEKS

● <u>Carnes Creek</u> - Discovered no later than 1865 and possibly as early as 1864, this placer creek flows into the Columbia River from the east side. It is located approximately 24 miles north of Revelstoke.

Hydraulicking on French Creek in the early days

THE BIG BEND

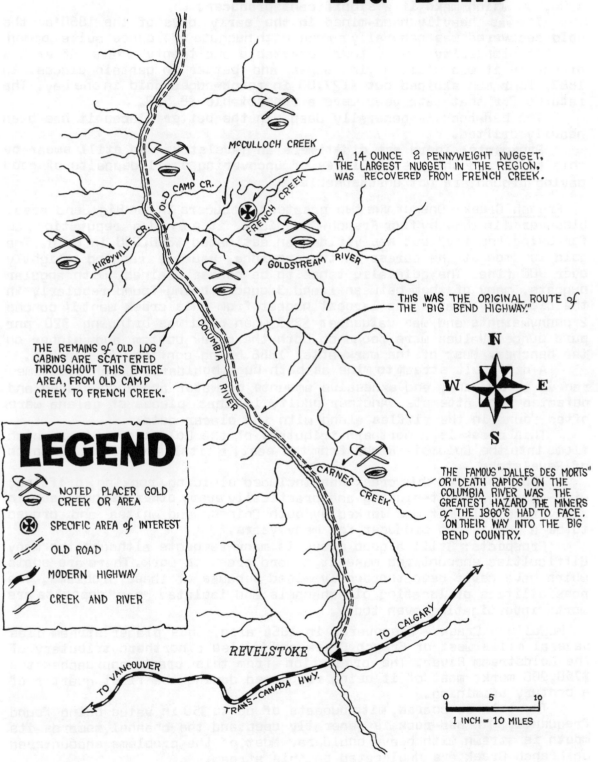

McCULLOCH CREEK

A 14 OUNCE 2 PENNYWEIGHT NUGGET, THE LARGEST NUGGET IN THE REGION, WAS RECOVERED FROM FRENCH CREEK.

OLD CAMP CR.

FRENCH CREEK

KIRBYVILLE CR.

GOLDSTREAM RIVER

THIS WAS THE ORIGINAL ROUTE of THE "BIG BEND HIGHWAY."

THE REMAINS of OLD LOG CABINS ARE SCATTERED THROUGHOUT THIS ENTIRE AREA, FROM OLD CAMP CREEK TO FRENCH CREEK.

COLUMBIA RIVER

N
W E
S

LEGEND

⛏ NOTED PLACER GOLD CREEK OR AREA

✠ SPECIFIC AREA of INTEREST

OLD ROAD

MODERN HIGHWAY

CREEK AND RIVER

CARNES CREEK

THE FAMOUS "DALLES DES MORTS" OR "DEATH RAPIDS" ON THE COLUMBIA RIVER WAS THE GREATEST HAZARD THE MINERS of THE 1860's HAD TO FACE, ON THEIR WAY INTO THE BIG BEND COUNTRY.

TO CALGARY

REVELSTOKE

TO VANCOUVER

TRANS-CANADA HWY.

0   5   10
1 INCH = 10 MILES

Although not as famous as either French or McCulloch creeks, this stream has produced an appreciable amount of placer gold over the years. The precise total is not known but the estimates range up to nearly $200,000 which make it a significant producer.

It was heavily hand-mined in the early days of the 1860's; the gold recovered was generally coarse with nuggets of ½ ounce quite common.

Its longevity was rather remarkable and twenty years after its discovery it was still paying wages and better in certain places. In 1887, four men sluiced out $127.00 in rough-edged gold in one day. The returns for that late year were a respectable $8,550.

The bed-rock is generally deep. In the better places it has been heavily drifted.

Prospects: There are old-timers in Revelstoke who still swear by this creek and the possibilities of uncovering small deposits of good paying ground are not unreasonable.

French Creek - One of the two greatest producers in the Big Bend area. Discovered in 1864 by four French-Canadians, it earned a reputation as for being "spotty" but has yielded an estimated $800,000 in gold. The gold is amongst the purest in the province, usually running slightly over 900 fine. The gold also tends to be coarse grained, with angular nuggets, many of them between 1 and 3 ounces being found regularly in the discovery years. The largest nugget from this creek went 14 ounces 2 pennyweights and was valued at $253 when gold was bringing $20 per pure ounce. Values were found on both the creek bottom and higher on the benches. Most of the work after 1886 being confined to benches.

A difficult stream to mine as both huge boulders, which sometimes ran up to 50 tons, and excessive amounts of water are encountered and defeated many attempts. Another oddity is that pieces of galena were often found in the riffles along with the placer gold.

This creek is a northern tributary of the Goldstream River which flows into the Columbia River from the east, a little over 50 miles north of Revelstoke.

The mining on this creek has included sluicing, rocking, drifting, wing-damming, shaft-sinking and practically every other method used in recovering gold. It was worked by both Chinese and whites and proved to be a consistent producer for many years.

Prospects: Still a good creek in many respects although the many difficulties encountered make it a hard creek to work. There are spots which have never been thoroughly mined because of these problems. The possibilities of locating old channels and isolated "pay" deposits are worth investigating even today.

McCulloch Creek - Discovered in 1864 also, this placer stream lies several miles west of French Creek and is also a northern tributary of the Goldstream River. The production from this creek approached the $750,000 mark; most of it being recovered during the first quarter of a century of mining.

The gold is coarse, with nuggets of up to $50 in value being found frequently. The bed-rock is generally deep and the channel towards its mouth is strewn with heavy boulders. Most of the problems encountered on French Creek are duplicated on this stream.

It was mined heavily in the 1860's, again in the 1885 to 1899 era and also in the 1930's. Somewhat "spotty" it nevertheless was a fairly consistent producer and was worked by hundreds of experienced miners and scores of companies, with varying degrees of success.

Prospects: Although many miners have tackled this creek and lived to rue it, it is still worth examining. There are many difficulties but because of these very problems the chances of occasional deposits of "pay" still remain.

Placer miner's cabin on McCulloch Creek in the Big Bend region. Notice the pick, shovel and gold pan outside.

CONCLUSION

"Thousand Dog Joe" and his dog-teams are seen no more on the trail to the gold creeks, and the years when the phrase "Big Bend" caused a ripple of excitement throughout the province has long since passed.

But there is still something appealing about this region, it may be the very remoteness of the placer creeks with the awesome Columbia rumbling close by, or the sheer magnificence of the scenery, whatever it is - it has that special uniqueness, a difference which will soon disappear with the completion of the hydro projects. So see it before it's too late.

XIV

OKANAGAN

INTRODUCTION

It is probable that Mission Creek, near Kelowna, in the Okanagan Valley, was found to be auriferous as early as 1856 by William Pion, a half-breed who was travelling between Fort Kamloops on the Thompson River and Fort Colville. Other creeks in the region, including Cherry (now Monashee) Creek, may also have been discovered to be gold-bearing at the same time.

By early 1861, the American miners strung out along Rock Creek in the Boundary Country heard rumours of a rich creek on the eastern side of Lake Okanagan. Soon after the news became common knowledge a party of veteran prospectors headed for the new diggings less than a hundred miles westward to determine for themselves exactly what the prospects were.

On March 1st, Adam Beam, who is credited with discovering the Rock Creek diggings, returned to that camp. On his return he stated to the Gold Commissioner:

> "We prospected nine streams, all tributaries of the lake and found gold in each averaging from three to ninety cents to the pan, the ground was much frozen and impeded our work. We are quite satisfied of the richness of these mines and shall as soon as is feasible dispose of our claims on Rock Creek and leave for that section of the country, where a miner can grow his potatoes and other vegetables, beside keep his cow. We hand you some gold taken from William Peon's claim. He makes $4 per day with a rocker and as ... old and practical miners (we) could realize more by sluicing and other methods.
>
> The Indians treated us most hospitably .... We only prospected the flats and frost preventing our prospecting up the creeks where it is naturally believed the principal portion of the gold is deposited."

Although Beam's expectations of the amount of gold in the creeks in the Okanagan were doomed to disappointment, there was gold in some of the creeks. The first stream of any consequence was a creek known as Riviere L'Anse du Sable, which flowed out of the hills to the east of Kelowna. But its placers were not rich and although several other streams emptying into Okanagan Lake were found to carry appreciable amounts of gold, none of them became significant producers.

About the same time a tributary of the Shuswap River called Cherry Creek was discovered. The gold was coarse and nuggets were plentiful. In the first years numerous white miners, many of them French-Canadians, recovered perhaps $90,000 in gold from this creek. Later, the Chinese moved in and mined it successfully for another decade or so. The gold from this creek carried a high percentage of silver and assayed out at a poor 712 fine. Soon after, another gold-bearing stream in the area, Harris Creek, was found to yield fairly heavily. It was the only part of the Okanagan which was to produce with any degree of consistency.

Today most of the Okanagan creeks lie abandoned although a few prospectors may be found occasionally along the south fork of Cherry Creek, a branch now known as Monashee Creek, and also on Harris Creek, some miles farther west.

On the other creeks like Mission, Whiteman, Bear and Nashwito, a few signs of former activity may be seen in isolated places along the creek bottoms, spots which miners like Gallagher and McDougall worked so many years ago, but generally few passersby even realize that these neglected streams were once considered promising placer creeks.

THE PLACER CREEKS

● <u>Cherry Creek</u> - Discovered to be gold-bearing around 1876, the most productive section of this creek was the South Fork which is presently known as Monashee Creek. The total yield from this creek is estimated to be around $125,000. The gold recovered is inclined to be coarse and runs only 712 fine. Nuggets of up to 8½ ounces have been recovered and specimens of ½ to 1 ounce were quite frequently encountered during the first decade of mining. The gold is usually found from about 4" above bed-rock down to that layer. It has been worked heavily and all of the old hand-mining methods, including wing-damming, were used. White and Chinese miners worked this creek.

Prospects: Probably the best of the Okanagan creeks. Some gold is still being sniped in various places along this creek and the chances of uncovering ground which was missed in the early years is relatively reasonable.

● <u>Harris Creek</u> - This stream lies several miles south of the village of Lumby in the north Okanagan. Although its pay section is quite short it has yielded excellent "pay" in certain areas. Miners like Fosbery did exceptionally well on this creek. The total production is estimated at close to $125,000. Unlike Monashee Creek, the placer gold from this stream is of high quality with nuggets and coarse gold commonplace.

Prospects: Although it has produced well in the past, because of its short length of paying ground, it must be considered fairly well mined out.

Some visitors to Cherry Creek standing in front of one of the original log buildings which once graced the first settlement known as "Cherry Creek Camp." This photograph was taken in 1926.

Mission Creek - This was the first placer creek of any distinction to be found in the Okanagan. It flows into Okanagan Lake from the east side several miles south of the city of Kelowna and was first known as Riviere L'anse au Sable. The best ground was found in and below the canyon which is located about 7 miles from its mouth.

Prospects: The reputation of this creek has been exaggerated by local residents although its total production may have reached the $50,000 mark, the gold was usually fine and nuggets rare. This stream has been well prospected.

Hydraulicking on Nashwito (Siwash) Creek on the west side of Lake Okanagan in 1925. This creek yielded an estimated $15,000 in gold.

CONCLUSION

There are places even today where, with a little luck, colours may be obtained and an occasional nugget recovered but those years when the Okanagan Valley was considered promising gold country have long passed.

Legends like the "Lost McLean Mine," still fascinate some of the local prospectors but the chances of finding a virgin creek is slim indeed.

XV

SIMILKAMEEN

Looking north from the "Treasure Cabin" in Granite City. Half a dozen
log structures still stand in this historic old placer camp which was
founded during the rush of 1885. Nearby, in Granite Creek, impressive
quantities of both gold and platinum were recovered.

INTRODUCTION

The Similkameen - Granite City, Blackfoot, Otter Flat; the names don't mean much today but there was a time when they did, in those days when the Similkameen Country was "poor man's diggings" and Granite Creek was the lodestar for placer miners.

It has a strange mining history, this part of the province, placer gold was known to exist there in some quantity as early as 1853 when one George McClelland found gold on the Similkameen near Vermilion Forks (Princeton) in that year.

From 1860 onwards, there was practically continuous mining by a number of miners like Sebastian Lotario, who bragged that "he had a bank on the river that he drew from whenever he was broke," and others like Billy Royal, the McKellop brothers and a number of Chinese. The mining, strangely, was carried on almost exclusively on the Similkameen River with very few attempts to test the Tulameen, so that placer rich river lay undisturbed for more than a quarter of a century.

Looking down the Tulameen. Sometimes spectacular results were obtained on this river which yielded quantities of both gold and platinum. This river was known as "spotty" whereas the Similkameen was known by miners as the "steady" river.

Finally, in the fall of 1885, a sometimes rustler and occasional prospector who went by the name of Johnny Chance; who was relegated to the menial task of cooking for a party of prospectors, made a discovery which resulted in the stampede of 1885 into the region.

Concerning this discovery, the diary of Mrs. Susan L. Allison, a long time residnet of the Similkameen states:

"Johnny Chance,...was too lazy to work....so he was sent out to get...a few grouse. He departed and strolled about till he found a nice cool creek which emptied itself into the river (Tulameen). Here, he threw himself down till sunset with his feet paddling the cool water, when a ray of light fell on something yellow. He drew it towards him, picked it up and found it was a nugget of pure gold. He looked into the water again and there was another, and another. He pulled out his buckskin purse and slowly filled it. Then, picking up his gun, he strolled back to camp where he became (known as) the discoverer of Granite Creek."

It was a time when the production of the other placer regions in British Columbia was on the wane so the result was a pell-mell rush to Granite Creek and the Tulameen River.

A solitary horse on the Dewdney Trail between the Similkameen valley and Hope. It was over this historic old trail that the miners of the 1880's streamed to get to Granite Creek.

The Deputy Provincial Secretary, Mr. Elwyn, visited the embryo camp at Granite Creek in that first year and reported:

"On the left bank, at the mouth of the creek, a level bench offers a good site for a town and is rapidly being covered with log houses. At the time of my visit there were seven general stores, two restaurants, two licensed houses for the sale of liquors and a butcher's shop. In addition, there were about fifteen houses in the course of construction. I estimated that there were between 400 and 500 white men and from 150 to 200 Chinese, on and in the neighbourhood of Granite Creek."

His report wasn't far out as the mining records show that there were 503 white miners and 195 Chinese working Granite Creek and the Tulameen River that year.

The placer gold production for that year surpassed the $100,000

"Checking for colours," the age-old practise of placer men everywhere. A nugget in the gold pan and the miner pauses to prospect the area more thoroughly.

mark and the next year it climbed to $203,000. The miners were puzzled to find another metal besides gold turning up in their sluice-boxes and rockers. This strange new metal was very hard, small grained, as heavy as gold, silver white in colour and lustrous. It was suspected that it was "platinum," a metal which was relatively unknown and unfamiliar to the miners then. Considered a nuisance by most of the miners who found the task of separating the two metals from each other during the clean-up, time consuming and highly annoying, it was called "poor man's gold" and was usually discarded. Platinum at that time "commanded 50¢ an ounce in Granite City," and sometimes sold at less than that. Never in their wildest imaginations did the miners anticipate that this despised metal would one day bring more than $400 a fine ounce. Only the Chinese, wise in so many ways, hoarded it and later profited mightily.

In a report dated December 24th, 1887, G. C. Tunstall, government Gold Commissioner at Granite City, wrote:

"I may mention that the production of platinum for the past season is estimated at 2,000 ounces...."

He went on to state that thousands of ounces of the metal had been thrown away by the white miners who were convinced that it was almost valueless. Decades later another generation of miners returned to the Tulameen to recover the once despised metal.

The 1887 season produced $128,000 in gold but thereafter the take

A little over half an ounce of gold from 10½ hours of sniping on bedrock on the Similkameen River. Worth more than $150 at today's prices it is proof that the old-timers didn't get all the gold. On an exceptionally good day an experienced sniper can snipe up to an ounce in ten hours if the water is low, usually in the early fall.

declined and continued to do so for the next seven years. Although the 1895 results improved somewhat with an estimated $50,000 production, the rush was over and by the turn of the century it was a dead camp. Granite City was finished too, and by 1915, after several disastrous fires had razed it, it was little more than a ghost town.

The total recorded production of the Similkameen-Tulameen area is approximately $765,000 with Granite Creek providing $450,000 of that. The recorded production, however, is misleading as there are no records of the amount taken between 1860 and 1885 and the region, especially the Similkameen River, was mined heavily in places, during those years by individual whites and companies of Chinese. It is probable that the actual yield was considerably more than $1,000,000 in placer gold. It should also be pointed out that an estimated 15,000 ounces of platinum were also recovered in its placers and this would add at least another $1,000,000 to the total. Quite a record for a relatively restricted area.

So, this out-of-the-way section of the province, where both gold and platinum are recovered in its creeks, has contributed much to the mining history of British Columbia.

And it is still an impressive area - and a walk through old towns like Tulameen, Coalmont and Granite City, brings to mind memories of those years when they were booming mining towns and hundreds of miners were tramping in over the Dewdney Trail to reach "Granite."

Even yet there is a lure to this area. You may not find the long lost "Platinum Cache" and it is unlikely that you'll discover another

The last days of Granite City - 1913.

gold creek as rich as Granite, but you won't forget this corner of the province - especially if you take the time out to wander through the quaint valley of the Tulameen where creeks with names like Slate and Boulder once drew hordes of restless argonauts to their banks.

THE PLACER CREEKS

● <u>Granite Creek</u> - This was the premier placer creek of the region with a recorded production of $450,000 although the actual take was probably between $500,000 and $600,000. Discovered in 1885 by Johnny Chance, there is some evidence that it was actually bypassed by Chinese miners prior to that year. This creek is a tributary of the Tulameen River and flows into it from the south near the village of Coalmont. The gold tends to be coarse and runs .875 fine. Nuggets from 2 to 4 ounces were commonplace in the early days and the largest specimen recorded weighed 10 ounces 5 pennyweights. The platinum production from this historic creek was remarkable and is estimated at close to 10,000 ounces. The platinum is fine grained although pieces up to ½ ounce have been found. Its history has included extensive hand-mining by whites and Chinese. In the 1890's it was also hydraulicked near its mouth.

Prospects: Hundreds of capable prospectors have worked this creek for years. There are sections which still give sniping returns and a few areas might bedrifted with interesting results.

Still a fascinating placer creek.

● <u>Lawless (Bear) Creek</u> - Also discovered in 1885, this creek was first known as Bear Creek. It is a tributary of the Tulameen and empties into that river west of the village of Tulameen. Although it never achieved a reputation like some of its neighbours, it did give up some astounding nuggets. In 1885 and 1886 three specimens recovered weighed 17, 23 and 24 ounces. The figures regarding its production are deceptively low as the total returns from the creek stand at $2,000. Surprising indeed, when the three nuggets previously mentioned make up more than half that amount. The explanation, of course, is that Lawless Creek was almost exclusively a "Chinese" creek and those enduring miners rarely gave out any information concerning their take, especially if it was good.

Prospects: Again a creek with a history of very coarse gold. It has, however, been well mined and the Chinese were not noted for missing much good "Pay."

Despite its chances it shouldn't be passed up.

● <u>Lockie (Boulder) Creek</u> - This creek flows into Otter Lake from the west and was discovered in 1885. Originally called Boulder Creek, it holds the record for the largest nugget ever found in the district when a Chinese miner uncovered a 52 ounce 5 pennyweight piece in 1887. The existance of this massive specimen was kept from the white miners of the Similkameen until Wells, Fargo and Company, the firm who had bought it from the Chinese, placed it on exhibit in their offices in Victoria.

Miner Gunnar Tjenner with half a pound of gold in the pan.

Cleaning bedrock on the Golden Gate claim on Granite Creek in 1913.

(136)

This creek was controlled by Chinese companies during its best productive years. The true production figures, therefore, are not known.

Prospects: Probably better than the majority of the other placer creeks in the district. The area close to the canyon was considered to be the most remunerative in the early years and deserves a look.

● Similkameen River - This river was found to be gold-bearing in 1853 and has been mined almost continuously since that year. The portion of the river which has received the most attention is from Princeton up-river to Whipsaw Creek. Both gold and platinum occur in some quantity although the gold is somewhat finer grained than elsewhere in the area. Nuggets weighing more than ½ ounce were unusual. Its total production is supposedly $100,000 although this is undoubtedly low because for a quarter of a century, from 1860 to 1885, there were no records kept.

Prospects: A few stalwarts are still mining on this river today, and snipers have done well in certain spots for years. There are even places where panning pays.

An interesting river indeed.

● Tulameen River - The precise discovery date is vague although the Tulameen was known to carry placer gold in 1860. It has a reputation for being "spotty" but has produced a recorded $150,000 which really is probably much higher. Worked by both Chinese and whites and some Fraser River Indians. There are some good sections which have produced prodigious quantities of both platinum and gold. The best area extends from 4 miles east of Granite Creek and on up-river to Britton (Eagle) Creek. The gold is finer than that found on its tributaries.

Prospects: The benches of the Tulameen have produced well in former years and there are sections which have never been well prospected. It is a river with miles of potential "pay" and should not be passed up.

Still worth looking at despite its "spottiness."

Other placer areas in the Similkameen:

Collins Gulch, Friday Creek, Hayes (Five Mile) Creek, Manion (Cedar) Creek, Newton Creek, Olivine (Slate) Creek, Saturday Creek, Whipsaw Creek.

CONCLUSION

The Similkameen is one of two areas in the world where both placer platinum and gold are obtained in quantity. Despite the proximity of the region to larger centers of population, it has remained generally isolated and has lost little of its natural charm and solitude. There are still places, even today, in the back areas of the Tulameen which have changed but little since the days of Podunk Davis, Bill Miner and Johnny Chance.

XVI

BOUNDARY

INTRODUCTION

Boundary - According to history, a nomadic Canadian named Adam Beam was supposedly the first man to find placer gold in Rock Creek in the Boundary country in 1859. There is, however, another and more romantic version concerning the discovery of gold in that creek. According to this story, two American soldiers were riding dispatch in 1858 and in order to avoid contact with hostile Indians in the southern part of the Okanagan valley, they circled north and followed the Kettle River for some distance and then rode in a westerly direction. Several miles from the river they came to a wide canyon which was passable only at one point. Guiding their horses along the canyon rim they slowly descended to the creek bottom where, as night was falling, they decided to make camp. Early the next morning, one of the soldiers, who had gone to the stream for water, noticed an unmistakable glint on the bedrock of the little creek, with high hopes he drew out the object which had caught his eye, and discovered that it was a nugget of gold. Quickly forgetting their orders, the soldiers stayed at the crossing for several days, and in that period gathered up a quantity of gold. Then, lacking both pans and shovels, they reluctantly continued on their mission. And that is how, according to the old account, Rock Creek was really discovered. Beam, it goes on, learned of their discovery some months later when the two messangers returned to Fort Colville. He in turn, made his way to the unnamed creek where he found placer gold and eventually gained the reputation as the discoverer of the creek.

Whether or not the unsubstantiated version is true, there is some evidence that Beam was not the first on the creek, for in 1859 one of the earliest worked and richest bars was designated "Soldiers Bar," a name by which it is known to this day.

Almost simultaneously with the discovery of Rock Creek, another stream close by was found to be gold-bearing, this creek, which also emptied into the Kettle River, came to be called Boundary Creek. By 1860 a full-fledged rush was under way and five hundred miners were in the district.

The activity was at its greatest in those first few years and an estimated $250,000 in gold was recovered from Rock Creek and another $100,000 from Boundary Creek.

Two mining camps also came into being, the most important was at Rock Creek and was known by that name. The Gold Commissioner, W. Cox, described it briefly in January, 1861:

"The town now contains twenty-three good houses, some of which have been erected at a large outlay."

The early mining camp of Rock Creek was a pretty crude affair and was inhabited by a host of disreputable characters, ranging all the way from sluice-box thieves to tin-horn gamblers. Cox, a resolute frontier "judge" dealt with them quickly and had soon rid the town of most of the undesirable elements - usually by simply giving them several hours

(139)

to "quit" the town or face a miners jury. The alternative was something less than pleasurable and the unwanted ones soon vanished to ply their dubious "trades" elsewhere. On more than one occasion, Cox and the Rock Creek miners assisted them on their way with an elaborate "drumming out" ceremony.

The other "town" in the Boundary at this time was at Boundary Creek and consisted of about half a dozen rough log cabins.

For nearly three years the returns held up and the area thrived. But when the production dropped so did the mining population and though several other smaller gold-bearing creeks were discovered, their yield was not enough to hold the prospectors. By the end of the decade the region was all but deserted.

It remained so until the 1890's when there was a brief revival with some hydraulicking, especially on Rock Creek, but the production was minimal and the area lapsed soon after. During the 1930's, when economic conditions made so many old areas look attractive, mining was carried on, and Rock, Boundary, McKinney and a few other placer creeks in the area came alive briefly once again.

Today, however, there are few prospectors in the old haunts and the creeks which knew the likes of Jimmy Copeland, Adam Beam, "Jolly Jack" Thornton and a hundred other characters, lie dormant.

The scars of these former operations still mark the valleys of Rock and Boundary creeks and occasionally, when a week-end panner turns up a nugget missed by those men of the past, those dim visions of the days when Rock Creek was booming, suddenly become much more vivid.

An abandoned log building above McKinney Creek. Beyond lies old Camp McKinney, the area where a hold-up man named Matt Roderick buried two gold bars in 1896, a treasure which has yet to be found.

THE PLACER CREEKS

● Boundary Creek - Originally known as "American" or "Ten Mile" Creek, this stream later became known as Boundary Creek and empties into the Kettle River near Midway. Discovered in 1859, it was mined heavily for some years after its discovery. Initially worked by whites, it later fell into Chinese hands. It has been hand-mined with reportedly good results and later wing-dammed and hydraulicked. Several excerpts from the letters of Gold Commissioner Cox indicate that it was a good gold creek. In 1860 that writer wrote:

"I visited the "Ten Mile" or "Boundary Creek" and found fifty men at work, very few of the claims are in active operation

Chinese miners at work hydraulicking on Rock Creek in 1895. In that year there was a brief flurry of activity on the creek after years of inactivity.

t those in full work yield from $20 to $35 per day to the
hand...."

The best "pay" on this creek ran from its mouth up-stream for
3 miles to the old Thornton claim. The gold is sometimes coarse and
nuggets up to 1½ ounces have been recovered. The bed-rock tends to be
soft and most of the gold is found on or close to this layer.
        Old Jack Thornton spent a longer time than any other miner on this
creek and and did fairly well at times.
        Prospects: Boundary Creek is inclined to be "spotty" but there
are sections which still bear investigation. The creek is fairly easy
to work although there are large boulders at depth in certain spots.
Snipers have done relatively well on occasion as there is visible bedrock in many places.
        Still an intriguing creek.

● Rock Creek - Known as "York" Creek initially, it soon became "Rock,"
and was the premier creek of the Boundary country. Its total estimated
production was well over the $250,000 mark. Worked by both whites and
Chinese, it had two distinct and separate "runs" of gold, one a lemon
yellow and the other a rusty copper colour. In many places coarse gold
was recovered and nuggets of 1 to 2 ounces were relatively common in
the first years. The largest nugget found on this creek was valued at $150.
Like most placer creeks it went through the hand-mining stages where
rockers and sluices were used. Later, both drifting and hydraulicking
were quite successful in various places. An estimated 500 miners were
on this creek in the early days and the results were, in some cases,
excellent. The old bars like Soldiers, Denver and White's, produced
quantities of placer gold and have been worked for more than a century
by a succession of miners. The famous "Rock Creek Rebellion" by miners
from the United States was staged on this creek. The original camp at
its mouth had a tough reputation with several murders occurring in the
vicinity, one of them remaining unsolved to this day.
        Prospects: Still good, despite the amount of work done along much
of its length. The benches probably offer the best chances of success
although the possibilities of finding old channels cannot be dismissed.
There are still areas where "pay" could be found although the barren
stretch between the upper and lower sections of the creek have never
produced much due to the depth to bedrock.
        A creek with many problems but deserves a look even today.

● McKinney Creek - Discovered in 1859, this little creek is a tributary
of Rock Creek and flows into the latter about 1 mile above the "Canyon"
bridge. This stream has produced some quantity of coarse gold and was
long worked by the Chinese after the white miners had abandoned it. It
varies from section to section and has been hand-mined and hydraulicked
extensively through most of its "pay" section.
        Prospects: "Spotty" today but a few local prospectors still feel
that it holds possibilities on some of the benches. The area worked in
the 1860's was from its junction with Rock Creek and on up-stream to
the mouth of Rice Creek.
        Panning still gets some results in selected spots but the chances
must be considered rather poor generally.

The gold camp of Rock Creek, B. C. in 1861

(Courtesy - Public Archives of Canada)

The remains of old Camp McKinney in 1928.

CONCLUSION

Traces of the historic old Dewdney Trail that "All Red Route" of yesterday still skirt the gold creeks where long days ago prospectors toiled for the "yellow metal." And along those famous streams of the past there are still reminders of those days of high hopes, decaying log cabins, forgotten claim posts and the occasional old grass-covered grave.

Even today the Boundary Country exerts a strange pull for those who have a feel for history. They are the ones found on those placer creeks of the past, panning out a few colours or ranging the country around old Camp McKinney, ever hopeful of stumbling across the "Lost Gold Bars" which were secreted so many years ago by strange Matthew Roderick.

Stand for a while on the rim of the canyon, high above old Rock Creek and gaze down at that once renowned placer stream, or dip your gold pan in Boundary Creek where forgotten multitudes mined so long ago, that's when you'll get the feel of the Boundary Country.

XVII

WEST KOOTENAY

The hotel at Seven Mile Point on the Pend d'Oreille River with some of the crew of the Pend d'Oreille Hydraulic Company posing in front of the hotel. This photograph was taken sometime in the 1890s when the company was active along the river.

INTRODUCTION

West Kootenay - This part of the province had barely been penetrated by the halfway mark of the 19th century. A few resolute trail-blazers had passed that way before that time, some intrepid Nor' Westers and a few of the servants of the Honourable Company, and although their stay had been brief, names like Boat Encampment and Pend d'Oreille remain to mark their passage.

Sometime in the 1850's, possibly 1855, a mountain man, whose name has long since been lost, discovered placer gold at the mouth of a river which emptied into the Columbia near the international boundary line. This river, which boiled out of precipitous canyon country to the east, was called the Pend d'Oreille. Before long, word of the find filtered down to old Fort Colville, and soon after the first band of prospectors were encamped at the scene of the discovery.

Even these tough adventurers, who were mostly Americans, were awe-struck by the dangerous river; for in those years before it was tamed somewhat by a series of dams, it was a raging and awesome sight.

The fatal lure of gold, however, spurred them on, and before long they were inching their way up the river, testing the bars and benches as they proceeded. By 1860, there were several score miners along the river. Soon, differences arose between the miners and the local Indian nations; the Lakes and the Kutenais. The miners were bent on exploring the country to the north and the Indians were equally adamant in their

A store in Waneta, near the mouth of the Pend d'Oreille River. Half of this store stood on Canadian territory and the other half in the United States - the boundary line ran through the center of the building. This particular photograph was taken sometime in the 1920's.

Prospector Matt Hill on his Indian pony "Bird," in the late 1890s.

The Pend d'Oreille plunging into the Columbia. The force of the current of the tributary is apparent in this photograph which was taken years ago.

determination to prevent the "Bostons" from penetrating farther into their hereditary territory. In the spring of 1861 an inevitable and bloody encounter took place in which a numerically superior band of heavily armed miners were repulsed by a warparty of Kutenai Indians; who were armed only with the formidable and famous Kutenai flat bows. In an effort to avert a repitition of the Fraser River Affair of 1858, the government dispatched Gold Commissioner William Cox to the scene. This troubleshooter was able to placate both sides and soon after the miners began exploring the streams farther inland.

Nearly 13 miles from the mouth of the Pend d'Oreille they found placer gold on a tributary known as the Salmon, this river joined the Pend d'Oreille from the north. Gold was found in quantity on several sections along this river, especially near its junction with the Pend D'Oreille, a number of its tributaries like Erie, Lost, Porcupine and Quartz were also gold-bearing. As the search was pressed farther north several more creeks rising out of the Bonnington Range were found to carry gold as both Hall and Forty-Nine creeks, both flowing into the Kootenay River west of Nelson, produced fine gold.

And farther north, beyond the head of Kootenay Lake, several new streams were discovered as both the Duncan River and Lardeau Creek received some attention for a few years; with a small rush occurring to the latter in the 1890's.

But the placer gold of the West Kootenay, except for those first few years of mining on the Pend d'Oreille, was never productive enough to hold the majority of the miners, and a decade later most had gone on to other fields like the Cariboo or the Big Bend. A few remained on the Pend d'Oreille, the Salmon and on creeks like Erie, but they were the exceptions and by 1900 most of the mining activity in the area had died down.

The old bridge across the Salmo River at the junction of the Salmo and the Pend d'Oreille. Two men are guiding the heavily laden pack-train across the bridge on their way to a placer mining operation a little way down the Pend d'Oreille. A turn of the century photograph.

THE PLACER CREEKS

<u>Erie Creek</u> – Discovered sometime after 1856 by American prospectors who came in from the Pend d'Oreille River. This stream flows south out of the Bonnington Range and joins the Salmo River near the town of Salmo. The canyon area was the most productive with both coarse gold and some fair sized nuggets recovered in that region. The placer gold was often found on a hardpan or on bedrock.

Prospects: Although never a great producer it did yield some gold to individual miners. There are places on this creek which could return interesting amounts of gold to a good prospector.

<u>Pend d'Oreille River</u> – Discovered to be gold-bearing in 1855, it was a fairly productive river in the early days. A difficult river to mine at any time because of its turbulence it did yield quantities of both fine and coarse gold. It was hand-mined extensively by numerous individuals and some companies and probably produced somewhere around $150,000 in the first three-quarters of a century. Much of the river today cannot be mined because of the hydro projects on the river.

Probably one of the most dangerous watercourses in the province in the 19th century it was never wing-dammed to any extent and even then was generally avoided by the Chinese who quickly realized that it was a tough river to make wages on.

Miners Matt Hill and Will Hayes examining placer gold in their pan on the historic Pend d'Oreille in the 1890s.

Prospects: The Pend d'Oreille is not nearly as remunerative as it once was and the hydro projects have inundated many good stretches of the river. There are a few places on the benches which should be well prospected for pay but the possibilities are limited. Although it was one of the first gold-bearing rivers discovered in the province it is less than promising. West Kootenay miners might be well advised to try other placer creeks in the region, the chances are better elsewhere.

Salmo (Salmon) River - A tributary of the Pend d'Oreille which flows into that river from the north, between Nelway and Waneta. Most of the early activity was confined to the section from its mouth upstream for several miles. The gold is somewhat coarse although nuggets above the 10 pennyweight size were rarely found.
Prospects: Interesting still. Some possibilities in the section from its mouth upstream. Crevices have yielded well in the old days, and could return results even now. It has been well prospected.

Other placer creeks in the area:

The Duncan River, Forty-Nine, Hall, Lardeau, Lost, Porcupine, Quartz and Rover creeks.

CONCLUSION

Although some of the old haunts of a century ago have changed, the scenery hasn't, it's still spectacular.
Old Fort Shepherd has been gone for a hundred years, razed by fire shortly after the rush to the Pend d'Oreille had subsided. And that river has changed too, tamed in places where today's dams have slowed its descent, but where it still runs unfettered, it's the roaring river it was in 1856, when even the most resolute miner must have hesitated before ascending it to prospect along its upper reaches.
But these places are the exceptions, for on those other gold creeks where miners like "Dirty Face" Johnson, "Dutch Charley," "Dancing Bill" and a host of others toiled, it is not much different now than it was then. The trails which they once trudged along on their way to the gold creeks are still discernible and still used, the placer creeks which they mined continue to yield some of the precious metal. This country is memorable territory. When you stand at the junction of the Pend d' Oreille and the Salmo rivers, you stand on the threshold of the past, this is the West Kootenay at its best.

XVIII EAST KOOTENAY

INTRODUCTION

East Kootenay — There is a time honoured miners' theory which asserts that any creek draining west out of the Rockies never contains gold. These old assumptions often prove true but in this case there are several exceptions — the most illustrious of which is the famous Wild Horse River in the East Kootenay country.

It was discovered in late 1863 by American prospectors on their way back to Idaho's Coeur d'Alene country after a disappointing foray into Findlay Creek, a placer stream 32 miles north of the Wild Horse which had been found by a half-breed earlier in the year but had been "spotty" and limited in pay-dirt.

On their return, like dedicated placer miners everywhere, they stopped to test the tributaries of the Kootenay River. Finally, at the mouth of a creek flowing out of a valley to the east and just south of where old Fort Steele stands today, they struck interesting colours and decided to prospect further up-stream. Their curiosity was justified for later on that same day they hit rich "pay-dirt" at the mouth of a canyon — and a great placer creek was born.

The mouth of the mountainous Wild Horse River valley as it appeared in 1910. Fisher Peak dominates the entire area where placer gold in great quantity was found in 1863 and led to the Wild Horse Rush.

The canyon of the Bull River below the "Pack Bridge," in 1926. The Bull, just south of the Wild Horse, was a noted gold producer in the 1860's.

    It was first known as "Stud Horse" or "Lone Horse" Creek but it went down in history as the Wild Horse of the Kootenays. And it was rich, exactly how rich will never be known, for, like the Similkameen, Rock Creek, Big Bend and the lower Fraser River in its early years, it attracted miners who were predominantly American in origin, men who were notoriously tight-lipped when it came to revealing their placer gold earnings. In the Cariboo, Omineca and elsewhere, the majority of the gold mined was banked with Victoria firms like the Bank of British Columbia, Wells, Fargo & Company or Macdonald's Bank, but on the Wild Horse almost all of the gold mined left the country in the private pokes of American miners, leaving, of course, no accurate record of the total yield from the creek.
    But it was a fabulous find and by the summer of 1864 its fame had spread so rapidly that 1500 prospectors were encamped in the valley alongside the creek. In that year too, a hodge-podge mining camp made up of rough log buildings, came into being. It was named "Fisherville."

EAST KOOTENAY

SHOWING THE WILD HORSE AND PERRY CREEK AREAS

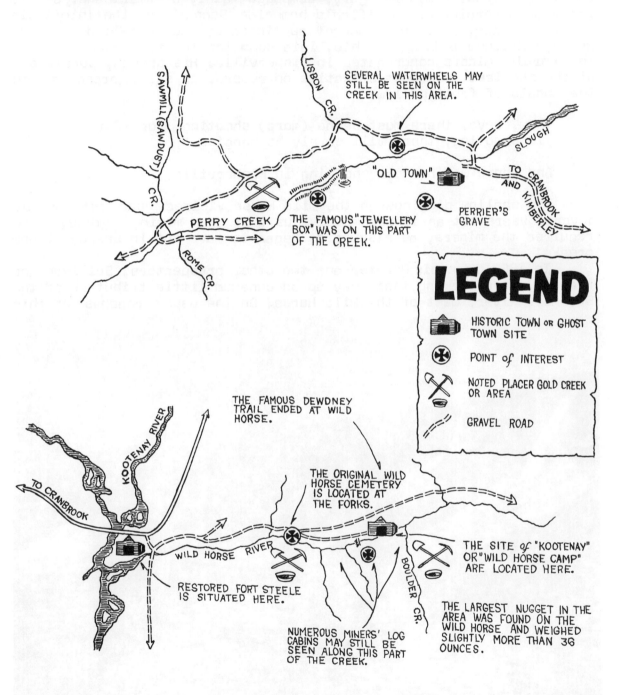

SAWMILL (SAWDUST) CR.

LISBON CR.

SEVERAL WATERWHEELS MAY STILL BE SEEN ON THE CREEK IN THIS AREA.

SLOUGH

"OLD TOWN"

TO CRANBROOK AND KIMBERLEY

PERRY CREEK

THE FAMOUS "JEWELLERY BOX" WAS ON THIS PART OF THE CREEK.

PERRIER'S GRAVE

ROME CR.

LEGEND

🏚 HISTORIC TOWN or GHOST TOWN SITE

✠ POINT of INTEREST

⚒ NOTED PLACER GOLD CREEK OR AREA

GRAVEL ROAD

THE FAMOUS DEWDNEY TRAIL ENDED AT WILD HORSE.

KOOTENAY RIVER

THE ORIGINAL WILD HORSE CEMETERY IS LOCATED AT THE FORKS.

TO CRANBROOK

WILD HORSE RIVER

THE SITE of "KOOTENAY" OR "WILD HORSE CAMP" ARE LOCATED HERE.

BOULDER CR.

RESTORED FORT STEELE IS SITUATED HERE.

NUMEROUS MINERS' LOG CABINS MAY STILL BE SEEN ALONG THIS PART OF THE CREEK.

THE LARGEST NUGGET IN THE AREA WAS FOUND ON THE WILD HORSE AND WEIGHED SLIGHTLY MORE THAN 36 OUNCES.

Named after one of the original discoverers, Fisherville quickly gained the reputation as one of the toughest gold camps in the Canadian west. It was in this camp that "East Powder Bill," a notorious renegade from Montana, shot and killed an Irishman named Tom Walker, in a shoot-out in a saloon. A miners' jury, composed mainly of Americans, calmly returned a verdict of justifiable homocide. Soon after, the inimitable Peter O'Reilly, a circuit "Judge" appointed by the so-called "Hanging Judge," Matthew Baillie Begbie, laid down the law to a mob of armed and unruly miners congregated in Fisherville. His speech, surely one of the shortest and most effective on record, is still preserved in the annals of frontier law:

>   "Now, boys, there must be no (more) shooting, for if there
>   is shooting, there will surely be hanging."

And there was no more shooting in Fisherville.

The shallow diggings on the Wild Horse yielded good returns for several years but as it became obvious that deep mining methods were required the miners, as elsewhere, began to move out in search of new creeks.

In 1867, Francois Perrier and two other prospectors, Sullivan and Kennedy, were working their way up an unnamed little tributary of the St. Mary River, west of the Wild Horse. On the upper reaches of this

The extensive hydraulic workings on the Wild Horse. The Chinese mining companies spent decades washing the rich gravels of this creek. The old tailings can still be seen at the base of the hillside.

creek, where the valley narrowed and the waters were swifter, the three
struck exciting "pay." The gold was coarse and much of it "seed-shaped."
Returning to the Wild Horse, the news of the new strike spread quickly,
and several days later hundreds of prospectors were hammering in their
claim stakes on the stream.

They were not to be disappointed with the new creek, for the gold
was found from the surface gravels down, and "shallow diggings" were
always the lone miner's friend. Most of the mining was confined to a
section barely several miles in length, and it was rich, especially
from the canyon on downstream about 1½ miles. The creek, first called
"Perrier's Creek," quickly became simply "Perry Creek." On a flat at
the lower end of the pay section, a mining camp known as "Old Town"
came into existence and it rapidly developed as the headquarters for
nearly one hundred and fifty miners. In those first years it boasted
two hotels, three stores, a crude jail and even a dance hall.

In that first decade Perry Creek produced an estimated $600,000,
and before this creek had run its course it had yielded an estimated
$1,000,000 in placer gold, a total surpassed only by the prolific Wild
Horse.

All too soon, however, the surface diggings became exhausted, and
only the deep miners were able to probe the golden gravels with success.
But they too were plagued by problems as quicksand and water defeated
many attempts. In places waterwheels were installed to cope with the
excess water, the deep miner's old enemy - and where they succeeded,
the take was rewarding, but these were isolated instances, and as the

a precarious bridge still used by prospectors on Perry Creek today. It
stands at the foot of the canyon, below the famous "Jewellery Box."

A strange message on Fox's mailbox. R. W. Fox was a semi-recluse who lived on the road to Old Town near Perry Creek. He passed on in 1940 but the mailman, unaware of his death, kept delivering his mail to the mailbox. Finally, almost a year later, another miner wrote: "DEAD about 1940" The mail came no more but the message remained and is barely discernible in this photograph.

The old Jordon over-shot waterwheel on Perry Creek in the East Kootenay. Ben and Mabel Jordon mined on this intriguing creek for years.

shallow ground became depleted, most of the miners moved on.

Farther to the west, the Moyie River and many of its tributaries were found to carry gold and the prospectors moved into that region. Those were the days when nearly all the creeks in the East Kootenay seemed to carry placer gold. North of the Wild Horse, Findlay Creek was yielding and so were neighbouring creeks like Toby, Dutch and Canon, and all added their share to the overall production.

Although the sixties was the golden decade, the returns were still significant for some years after. On through the 1880's and the 1890's, both white and Chinese miners continued to work on creeks like Perry, Wild Horse, Weaver and Findlay. In many instances their efforts were amply rewarded. Several excerpts from the early Mining Reports bear this out.

In 1888, Gold Commissioner Vowell reported:

"Mr. Leonard, a miner of great perseverance, who has stuck all alone to this creek (Weaver) for years, has taken out during the past season about $5,000 in coarse gold."

And despite extensive mining, the Wild Horse continued to pour out its riches. Ten years after it had been discovered, there were still 75 miners active along this creek. As late as 1895 the Reports stated:

"....the year 1895 was fairly successful on Wild Horse Creek, as from that creek alone the yield was $22,500 and prospecting of further ground was actively carried on."

By the turn of the century, however, there were only a few of the originals left, some still doing well, like old Dave Griffith on the

Bruce's old assay office on Perry Creek in 1926.

Wild Horse or Jack Thompson on Perry Creek. But the returns continued
to dwindle and by 1914 the placer gold production had slipped to $1,000.

There were many other mining operations afterwards but they never
approached the frenzied activity of those early years. A few Chinese
like Kee Chin continued to work the gravels of the Wild Horse and some
miners were on other creeks, like the Jordons on Perry Creek – but the
heyday had gone.

THE PLACER CREEKS

● Moyie River – Probably the third best area in the region as far as
total output is concerned. Somewhere around $175,000 in gold came from
this river and its gold-bearing tributaries like Weaver Creek, Palmer
Bar Creek and Negro (Nigger) Creek. One of the best areas was below the
falls on the upper river where tunneling in the 1930's resulted in good
returns. The gold found was generally finer than that of either Perry
or Wild Horse but nuggets of $5 in value and occasionally more were
sometimes picked up.

Prospects: Although this river hasn't the rich history of many of
the other placer creeks in the region, it is one of the rivers which
has not been thoroughly prospected. Some experienced local placer men
who are familiar with this river feel that the chances are fairly good
in respect to locating old channels on the Moyie or on one of its many
gold-carrying tributaries.

Certainly worth investigating.

● Perry Creek – Undoubtedly the second greatest placer gold creek in
the East Kootenay. Discovered in 1867 by Francois Perrier, this stream
flows into the St. Mary River and is located to the north-west of the
city of Cranbrook. Although its total production is uncertain, it has
probably produced in the neighbourhood of $1,000,000, as most of the
returns in the best years were not declared. A fascinating creek in
many respects with the most celebrated place on the creek known as the
"Jewellery Box," below which the richest part of the stream was found.
The gold recovered there was "tear-drop" shaped because of the action
of the water in the canyon or "Jewellery Box" section. Perry Creek was
actively mined for decades, from the site of "Old Town" and on up-stream
for nearly five miles. It was rich from grass-roots to bed-rock with
much of the gold being coarse. The purity of the gold from this creek
is exceptionally high, often running more than 920 fine. a number of
difficulties were encountered along this stream, the most prominent of
which were quicksand and excessive water.

Prospects: Like most good gold creeks, it has been well worked but
there are still places where sniping yields interesting results and a
few sections which warrant further prospecting for ancient channels.
An indicator of gold on this creek is the occurrence of a black rock
called "ironstone," and where it is found, gold is also.

A stream as intriguing as Perry Creek should not be bypassed. Some
interesting possibilities still remain.

The Gamble Mining Company's flume sluice-box on the Wild Horse River, 1918. This photo was taken after the clean-up was completed.

The hotel at Old Town on Perry Creek as it looked in 1926. Gus Thiess, an old-timer of the area is sitting on the porch.

● <u>Wild Horse (Creek) River</u> - First discovered by American miners on their return from Findlay Creek in 1863, this stream was initially known as Stud Horse or Lone Horse Creek. It flows out of a mountain valley on the east side of the Kootenay River near old Fort Steele. It was the foremost placer stream in the East Kootenay and its total yield eclipsed the combined production of all the other placer creeks in the East Kootenay region.

The estimates of the returns from this river have run from as low as $1,000,000 to as high as $30,000,000. The former figure is too low and the latter far too generous. Considering the number of miners who worked this river and the number of decades it was mined, it probably yielded somewhere around $7,000,000. There were only a handful of gold creeks in the province which were mined longer and these few are in the Cariboo and Atlin districts. The periods of greatest activity on this creek were in the first five years, 1863 to 1868, and again from 1885 to 1900. It was hand-mined with rockers and sluices and hydraulicked extensively after the shallow diggings had been depleted. The gold was coarse, with nuggets of 1 to 4 ounces quite usual in the 1860's. The largest nugget of record was recovered by one Mike Reynolds, a piece which weighed 36 ounces. Its gravels were so rich that the first camp which was called "Fisherville" was torn down so that the miners could work the ground on which it stood.

Prospects: Although it is a renowned placer river, it has been mined so thoroughly that the chances of locating any new deposits of "pay" are slim. In some places the bed-rock, which was notoriously soft, was penetrated to a depth of several feet in order to recover the gold. Any stream which has been mined this extensively cannot be considered too promising despite its history.

Other placer creeks in the area:

The Bull River, Boulder, Dutch, Findlay, Gold, Negro (Nigger), Palmer Bar, Porcupine, Quartz, Toby and Weaver Creeks.

CONCLUSION

Across that majestic river called the Kootenay, on past old Fort Steele and up into the Wild Horse. When you walk in this country, myriad ghosts of the past walk with you - the forgotten Chinese and their white counterparts like "Pleasant" Smith and "Old Bob" Dore, for this was a river where a thousand miners sluiced the gravels in their never-ending quest for gold. You won't forget the Wild Horse.

And westward, along the barely discernible trail up old Perry Creek, past the ruins of "Old Town," and still standing waterwheels which haven't turned these many years, skirting abandoned log cabins, their doors still ajar, waiting for the return of the argonauts who once ruled the creek. Stop at the foot of the canyon where the falls, unchanged and awesome, still guard the "Jewellery Box," of old. These are the memories of Perry Creek.

And this is the East Kootenay, the land of a thousand yesterdays, it remains an indelible country.

XIX
VANCOUVER ISLAND

The Berks Hotel on the Leech River, Vancouver Island, in the early 1860s.

INTRODUCTION

Vancouver Island – This part of the province is not usually regarded as a placer gold region yet there are a surprising number of creeks and rivers on the island which carry placer gold.

The most prominent of the placer rivers is the Leech. The gold on this river was discovered in 1864 by Lt. Peter John Leech, the astronomer for the Vancouver Island Exploring Expedition. In the first two years an estimated $100,000 was taken, and on the strength of this, several mining camps sprang up in the region. The most well known of these was called "Leechtown."

The Leech River placers, although short-lived, probably produced a total amounting to close to $175,000 with nuggets ranging up to one ounce in size being recovered. The largest nugget on record, weighed between four and five ounces and was recovered in 1864.

Although the Leech was the most conspicuous placer gold stream on the island it was not the first to be discovered. Several others pre-date it. One, China Creek, which was found in 1862, produced somewhere

Miners in front of the W. Ward & Company store on the Leech River in the early 1860s. The stock consisted on the basic necessities plus a liberal stock of liquor.

between $40,000 and $50,000 in its life. It was, as its name indicates, discovered and worked primarily by Chinese miners.

Another placer river, the Bedwell, was also discovered in 1862. It too, was mainly worked by Chinese who were diligently gleaning its gravels more than thirty years later.

The geological formation known as the "Leech River Formation," gives rise to nearly two-thirds of the gold-bearing streams on the island. Nearly all of these streams flow westward from this formation.

There are several other interesting placer gold areas on the island and one of these is the "Wreck Bay" area, now known as Florencia Bay, located on the west coast of the island just north of Ucluelet. This region has produced at least $35,000 worth of fine gold. The origin of the gold, however, is quite unusual as it occurs in the black sands of the beach, the gold being deposited there by the action of the Pacific Ocean, especially after heavy storms.

Most of the creeks on Vancouver Island were worked out by the turn of the century although there are several areas where desultory mining is still carried on.

So, Vancouver Island, generally assumed to be completely barren of placer gold, has a placer mining history like many other areas in British Columbia. Even at the present time, it is possible to wander along some of the western waterways and pan out "colours" where the prospectors of more than a century ago laboured.

Some "forty-niners" in front of Alley & Co.'s store on the Leech.

THE PLACER AREAS

• <u>Bedwell River</u> - This old placer river is located north and inland from Tofino and flows westward into Bedwell Sound. It was discovered in 1862 and was a favourite placer river of the Chinese, who worked it until the late 1890's. The production was estimated at somewhere around $40,000 in fine grained gold.

Prospects: Well worked by the Chinese who usually didn't miss much. Sniping could still result in some gold being recovered.

• <u>China Creek</u> - Reputedly the first significant placer creek found on the island in 1862, it was worked almost exclusively by Chinese. It empties into Alberni Inlet approximately 7 miles south of Port Alberni.

Prospects: This stream has produced between 2,000 and 3,000 ounces of fine placer gold but was heavily mined by the Chinese for years. "Colours," however, can still be obtained in places.

• <u>Leech River</u> - Still the most promising placer gold stream on the island. The quality of the gold was coarser and more plentiful on this river than on any other stream in the region. It has been hand-mined by rocker and sluice since its discovery in 1864 and was hydraulicked and drifted later. In the last few years it has even been worked by skin divers with dredging equipment. In latter years a number of ½ ounce and 1 ounce nuggets and other coarse gold have been found by snipers.

This river is located west of Victoria and empties into the Sooke River which also carries placer gold, although considerably finer than its tributary, the Leech.

Prospects: It has been well gone over by good miners for many years but snipers have been getting gold from it and will probably continue to do so for some time to come.

• <u>Wreck Beach</u> - This is one of the most well known beach placers in the province and is now known as Florencia Bay. It is situated about five miles north of Ucluelet. It has been worked for years and in one three year span, from 1899 to 1901, nearly 1,400 ounces of very fine gold was recovered from the black sands of the beach.

Prospects: A difficult area for novices to work because the separation of the gold from the black sands of the beach present special problems which are very hard to cope with. It would be wise to leave this area to the specialists.

• <u>Zeballos River</u> - Discovered to be gold-bearing well before the turn of the century, this up-island river flows west and is found near the town of Zeballos, which was once noted for its lode gold deposits.

Prospects: This river has a reputation as being "spotty." The best bets would probably be either sniping or panning.

"Layzell's Retreat" and several other tent stores on Kennedy Flat on the Leech River in 1864. At one time there were several hundred placer miners scattered throughout the area. Although the placers were generally poor one nugget weighed more than one-third of a troy pound.

CONCLUSION

Although the alluvial gold deposits of Vancouver Island were never famous for their richness - their total production probably amounted to only 20,000 ounces - they are rather numerous. In one 35 mile stretch on the west side of the island, from Port Renfrew south to the Sooke River, there are quite a number of gold streams, including the Gordon River, the San Juan, the Sombrio, Loss creek, the Jordan, the Leech and the Sooke. All of these flow westward and all have their origin in the old "Leech River Formation," from which so many of the island's placer streams flow.

There are few promising areas left but many of these historic gold streams still yield varying quantities of placer gold, from small nuggets and slugs to finer "colours." It is not likely that there are many nuggets remaining which are the size of the $70.00 specimen found on the Leech River in 1864, but nearly any novice can still recover fine gold in those old haunts once frequented by the Chinese and white miners of a century ago.

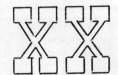

EQUIPMENT

1. <u>Free Miner's Certificate</u> - This is a permit required before the individual is allowed to stake a recognized Placer Mining Lease. The following requirements must be met: the applicant, with one or two exceptions, must be a Canadian citizen 18 years of age or older. A fee of $5 is paid to the Provincial Government Agent, Gold Commissioner or Deputy Recorder. The certificate is valid from the date of issue to the year end (December 31st). Old age pensioners are exempt from paying the $5 fee. Any person who qualifies may obtain a Free Miner's Certificate from a provincial government office. It is wise to carry your Free Miner's Certificate in your wallet on prospecting trips.

2. <u>Gold Pan</u> - There is a wide variety of gold pans available to the panner as most hardware and general stores stock this item. Nearly all experienced placer miners have their own favourite types of gold pans, which they invariably swear by. The majority of them are also inclined to denigrate types of pans that they don't use. Generally, a novice would be wise to choose a pan carefully because the first pan chosen is invariably the type used forever after. A metal gold pan is considered preferable to a plastic pan because the latter is inclined to split or break at the most inopportune time. A metal pan with "riffles" or "ridges" is probably the best for several reasons: they are easier to work with and considerably faster and because of the "riffles" they are inclined to save both fine gold and nuggets more easily than a standard pan. Prices range from as low as $3.95 for a 9" pan (nothing smaller should be used by a working miner) to about $6.95 for a larger 15" pan (which is preferable). Metal pans, if new, should be carefully burned on the inside before use. This is necessary because new pans are coated with a protective layer which must be burned off. The burning also darkens the bottom of the pan, ennabling the panner to see any gold in the pan much easier. A gold pan, in a pinch, may be used as a washbasin, a frying pan, a bucket or for a variety of other uses but despite its versatility it is the only piece of mining equipment which can accurately assess the value of potential placer ground.

3. <u>Miner's Pick</u> - A miner's pick differs somewhat from an ordinary pick in that a placer pick-head is slimmer and considerably lighter than the head of a standard pick. In the early years placer miners from different regions of the province tended to use different types of picks. In the East Kootenay country, on both Wild Horse and Perry creeks, a pick which was sharpened on one end and had a hammer head on the opposite end, was often preferred. In the Cariboo, Boundary, Atlin, Cassiar, Similkameen and most other mining districts in the province a "2 pound" pick head was used, sometimes with a protective steel shank. Today miner's picks are hard to come by although a few stores and mining outfitters carry them. A coal miner's pick head is almost the same as a placer miner's pick and a few are still found in the historic coal mining areas of the province such as Vancouver Island, Fernie and Merritt. Prices vary sharply for any decent pick. Occasionally a good placer pick can be found in a second hand store or in an auction for as little as $3 or $4. More often the price is $9 or more. A good pick should last for years but it should be kept sharp to ensure maximum efficiency. Anyone who has an original gold miner's pick should count themselves fortunate indeed, especially if it has a steel shank.

4. <u>Round-nosed Shovel</u> - A good shovel, is of course, a necessity. A round-nosed type is specified because a flat-nosed shovel cannot be used effectively by a placer miner in most situations. The standard round-nosed shovel will probably serve the purpose although several points should be considered when buying one. It should have a standard length handle and the handle should be carefully examined to see if it's straight-grained (it should be). The head of the shovel can also be checked to see if it is heavy enough to withstand the work. Sometimes a smaller and lighter shovel is used, but usually only when sniping, otherwise stick with a standard shovel. The prices of this piece of equipment varies from about $3 to as high as $18. A person shouldn't skimp on a shovel and never use it as a pry-bar.

5. <u>Knee-high Rubber Boots</u> - This item is also mandatory. Rare indeed is the placer man who doesn't own at least one good pair of rubber boots. They'll pay for themselves in comfort in a day's mining and they should last at least a season unless used continuously. Mining in cold feet is no fun so purchase a pair. Unfortunately, the prices have risen dramatically in the past four or five years and a good pair now costs anywhere from $8 to $11. Generally considered a must. Available practically anywhere in the province.

6. <u>Packboard or Packsack</u> - On even short trips it is a good idea to carry all mining equipment in either a packsack or on a packboard. On trips of under ten miles a packsack will usually do but on trips of several days duration a packboard (which carries more and is far more comfortable) should be chosen instead. Before purchasing either of these items it would be advisable to take the time to examine the workmanship and the material to see whether both will stand the use it will get. Prices of packsacks range from $5 up to well over $40. Packboards are far more expensive and should only be considered if serious prospecting is contemplated. Above all make sure that the harness is comfortable.

7. <u>Matches and Compass</u> - A relatively inexpensive pair of items but both should be kept waterproof in case of a fall in either a river or a creek. Matches in a waterproof container run about $3 and are well worth the price. A BIC lighter is always dependable. A fairly decent compass can be purchased for around $8 if you shop carefully. A miner should never venture out without these two items.

8. <u>Small Plastic Bottle</u> - Available for about 15¢. Used for storing fine gold, coarse gold and nuggets. The handiest size is about 2" by ¾" and should have a lock-top to safeguard against the top slipping off unnoticed (most annoying if it's full of gold). This, although inexpensive, is an item which should always be carried.

9. <u>Brass Gold Tweezers</u> - Choose tweezers which have curved points, not straight, unless you have no choice. Brass tweezers are the best because they don't magnetize. A handy tool for extracting gold from the pan or nuggets from crevices and cracks in bedrock. Some of the old miners (especially snipers) have a loop welded on their tweezers and hang them from a leather thong around their necks (so that they are handy and they don't lose them). The prices range from a low of $1 to as high as $5. A specialist's tool.

10. <u>Pry Bar or Breaking Bar</u> - Both of these tools are most useful but a pry bar is almost a necessity whereas a breaking bar is usually in use only when a miner is working in water or dredging. A good pry bar is usually about 4½ to 5 feet_long and heavy enough to move a several hundred pound rock. The C.P.R. provided most of the bars in the early days (gratis) but otday a good pry bar is tough to find. Prices (if you can locate one) run from about $18 to around $35. Occasionally a scrap metal dealer will have one. Any pry bar under 3 feet in length should be bypassed because a short bar doesn't have the leverage that a longer bar has. Breaking bars, on the other hand, are primarily a specialist's tool and are generally used only by placers miners who are dredging. They are almost always made up in a welding shop. The prices usually run from $30 and up. A good pry bar is very handy for a serious placer miner; a breaking bar for a dredger.

11. <u>Area Map</u> - This item is almost invaluable and should always be taken on trips, especially to unfamiliar districts. The best maps, with a scale of one inch to two miles, are the Department of Lands, Forests and Water Resources maps, which are available at practically all of the Provincial Government offices in the province for $2 each plus tax. Each map in the series, which covers the entire province, is coded by numbers and letters and covers nearly 1,500 sq. miles of territory. Anyone purchasing these maps from the Provincial Government offices should also check the local Placer Mining map of that district to determine which, if any, placer leases are open. This is wise because otherwise you may be trespassing on someone's lease.

12. <u>Whisk</u> - The sniper's friend. A good whisk can, and usually does, more than pay for itself in an afternoon's mining. Any placer miner who regularly cleans bedrock always has at least one whisk. Novices are usually surprised when they see an old hand carefully brushing bedrock dirt into a pan, but they're more surprised when they notice the amount of gold panned out from that dirt. The bristles on whisks are important, they should be fairly stiff, and they should not be more than 6" long, other wise they don't clean the bedrock as well as it should be cleaned. Necessary and costs only 75¢ to $3.00.

13. <u>Crevicing Tools</u> - There is a bewildering number of these tools. Used primarily by snipers (crevicers) for cleaning bedrock cracks and crevices, they are fashioned in such a way that they are capable of penetrating narrow cracks in bedrock where coarse gold and nuggets often lie. Made of good steel and kept unusually sharp by experienced placer miners, a crevicing tool is invaluable, especially where the bedrock is cracked and broken. There are only a few crevicing tools available in retail stores and few of these seem to be satisfactory. Most miners fashion their own or have them specially made. Sniping tools run from about $1 (for a thin screwdriver) to as much as $20. Anyone possessing an old crevicing tool in good condition is lucky.

14. <u>Gold Scales and Troy Weights</u> - Almost required equipment for any placer miner obtaining more than two ounces of gold each season. A set of modern hand-held scales costs anywhere from $20 to $60 or more whereas a precision balance scales in the lower price range usually costs from $80 to as much as $500. Any gold scale should come with a set of troy weights (troy ounces, pennyweights and grains) as gold,

platinum and silver are all weighed in the troy system in the West, and sales are usually made in the same system (in North America). A set of gold scales (with troy weights) can be bought from stores or dealers who specialize in mining equipment. Anyone possessing a set of old gold scales should retain them as they are becoming hard to come by. Any missing weights can be replaced.

15. Axe - One of the handiest tools of the miner. A standard single-bitted type can also double as a hammer in a pinch. This particular tools has many uses: cutting firewood, clearing brush, cutting tent pegs, squaring claim posts, etc. Prices range from a low of about $7 to well over $20. Always take your axe but never lend it.

16. Claim Tags - Tags are required by law if any Free Miner wishes to stake a Placer Mining Lease (PML) in the province. The tags come in pairs with matching numbers (one for the Initial Post and one for the Final Post) and may be obtained from any Provincial Government office for 50¢ a pair. Experienced miners usually carry two sets in case they come across ground they wish to stake.

17. Food - A specialized category which should be considered before embarking on prospecting trips of more than two or three days length. Staple items like salt, sugar, flour, tea and bacon should always be included and a complete list of food items should be drawn up well beforehand. An important category and items should be checked off as they are packed.

18. Clean-up Pan - Experienced placer men usually have a small gold pan which they use exclusively in cleaning up. A clean-up pan is a 9" or 10" pan usually. Sometimes a sniper (or crevicer), instead of panning down every pan of paydirt (a time consuming process) simply pans the concentrates down to the blacksand and dumps the residue, which usually contains fine gold and nuggets) into his small clean-up pan. After about twenty or thirty pans have been handled in this way the panner then pans out the contents of the clean-up pan. This process may be repeated several times a day and saves time.

19. Magnet - Generally a handy piece of equipment because a magnet can be used to separate the gold from the blacksand (magnetite). The blacksand is dried and then placed on a stiff piece of fairly heavy paper. The magnet is then placed under the paper and drawn along. The moving magnet attracts the blacksand, leaving the gold behind. This process does not always work when platinum is present with the gold in the blacksand (as it is in the Similkameen - Tulameen District), because nearly half of the platinum in British Columbia is magnetic and will be lost with the blacksands if a magnet is used. A magnet should be used only when platinum is not present. Suitable magnets can be purchased from anywhere from $1.50 to $5.00.

20. Miscellaneous - Under miscellaneous may be included items like first aid kits, flashlights, sleeping bags, knife, hammer, rope, an extra change of clothes, extra flashlight batteries, extra matches, cooking utensils, nails, tape measure and so on. The items in this category are important and should be checked off as they are packed so that they aren't forgotten.

XXI

MINING LAW

Regulations: The Placer Mining Act, Affidavit for Placer Lease, Affidavit on Application to Record Work, Bill of Sale of Mineral Claims, Miscellaneous Items and the Characteristics of Gold.

PLACER MINING ACT REGULATION

Interpretation

1. In this regulation,

"Act" means the *Placer Mining Act;*

"final post" means a legal post placed at the end of the location line where the location is completed;

"initial post" means a legal post placed at the point from which the location line is commenced;

"intermediate post" means a legal post placed at the point where the direction of the location line changes;

"legal post" means an initial, final, or intermediate post marked in accordance with this regulation;

"location line" means the straight line between the initial and final posts where an intermediate post is not used, but where an intermediate post is used the location line is the straight line between the initial post and intermediate post and the intermediate post and the final post;

"witness post" means a post used to indicate the position of a legal post.

Size and Shape of a Location

2. (1) The boundaries and area of the location shall be determined by establishing its end lines running from or through the initial post and from or through the final post, at right angles to the course of the location line at these posts respectively; and by establishing its side lines parallel to the course or courses of the location line.

(2) The maximum size of a location shall be 500 m × 1 000 m where the location is a straight line, and the following diagrams illustrate applications of subsection (1) and this subsection:

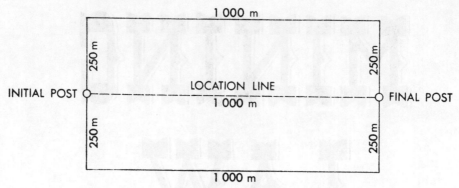

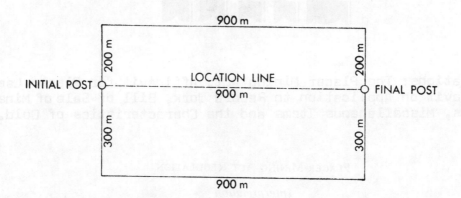

(3) Where the location line changes direction, the length of the location line shall not exceed 1 000 m and the following diagram illustrates an application of subsection (1) and this subsection:

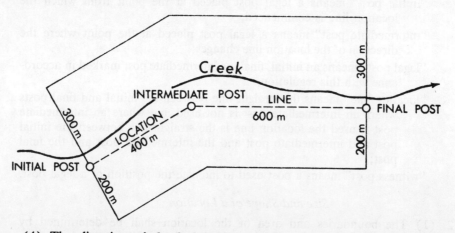

(4) The direction of the location line shall not change more than once throughout its length.

Staking a Location

3. (1) A legal post shall consist of

   (*a*) a piece of sound timber, firmly affixed to the ground, standing upright, not less than 1 m above the ground, squared and faced on four sides for at least 25 cm from the top, each face of the squared or faced portion measuring at least 89 mm across; or

   (*b*) a stump or tree cut off not less than 1 m above the ground and squared or faced as described in paragraph (*a*); or

   (*c*) a cairn of stones not less than 1 m in height above the ground.

(2) A witness post shall be the same dimensions as a legal post.

(3) A location shall be marked on the ground by the staker by

   (*a*) placing an initial post at the point from which the location line is commenced;

   (*b*) affixing to that side of the initial post which faces in the direction of the location line extending from the initial post a metal tag in the following form, embossed "initial post" and impressing on it the following information:

   (i) The name of the staker:

   (ii) If applicable, the name of the person for whom the staker is acting as agent:

   (iii) Date of staking:

   (iv) Direction to intermediate post (if one is used) or direction to final post (where there is no intermediate post):

   (v) Metres to right:

   (vi) Metres to left.

TAG NO. P_____

PLACER − INITIAL POST

STAKED BY_____

AS AGENT FOR_____

DATE_____

DIRECTION TO −
INTERMEDIATE POST
              OR   _____
FINAL POST

METRES TO RIGHT_____

METRES TO LEFT_____

   (*c*) marking the location line by blazing standing trees on two sides approximately facing the No. 1 or No. 2 post and by cutting underbrush or by marking the line between the posts in as permanent a manner as conditions permit, so that, from each mark on the line, the next mark on the foresite is visible and similarly, the last mark on the backsite is also visible.

   (*d*) placing an intermediate post, if the location line changes direction, at the point of change in direction of the location line and clearly, legibly, and durably marking it "intermediate post" and with the following information:

(i) The name of the staker:

(ii) If applicable, the name of the person for whom the staker is acting as agent:

(iii) Date of staking:

(iv) Direction to final post; and

(v) Distance from initial post;

(e) placing a final post at the end of the location line where the staking is completed;

(f) affixing to that side of the final post, facing in the direction of the location line extending from the final post, a metal tag in the following form embossed "final post" and impressing on it the following information:

(i) The name of the staker:

(ii) If applicable, the name of the person for whom the staker is acting as agent:

(iii) Distance from intermediate post (if one is used) or distance from initial post (where there is no intermediate post):

(iv) Date and time staking completed.

TAG NO. P_____

PLACER – FINAL POST

STAKED BY_____

AS AGENT FOR _____

DISTANCE FROM—
INTERMEDIATE POST
OR _____
INITIAL POST

DATE COMPLETED_____

TIME COMPLETED_____

Marking Legal Post by Witness Post

4. Where, because of prevaling topographical conditions, it is impossible for a staker of a location to place a legal post in accordance with section 3, the legal post may be marked by

(a) placing a "witness post" in a conspicuous place as close as practical to where under normal conditions the legal post would have been placed;

(b) clearly, legibly, and durably marking that site of the witness post which faces in the direction of the legal post being witnessed, with the distance and true bearing to the true position of the legal post; and

(c) affixing to that side of the witness post which faces in the direction of the legal post being witnessed a metal tag embossed "initial post"

Page five of the Placer Mining Act Regulation

or "final post" as the case may be and impressing the information required under section 3,
and the following diagram illustrates the application of this section:

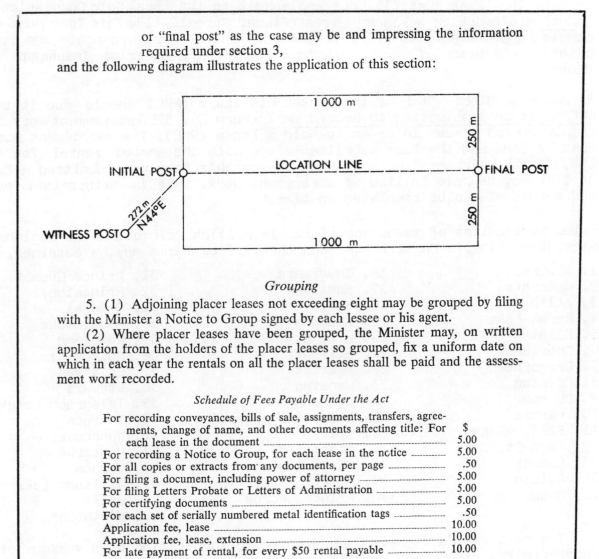

Grouping

5. (1) Adjoining placer leases not exceeding eight may be grouped by filing with the Minister a Notice to Group signed by each lessee or his agent.

(2) Where placer leases have been grouped, the Minister may, on written application from the holders of the placer leases so grouped, fix a uniform date on which in each year the rentals on all the placer leases shall be paid and the assessment work recorded.

Schedule of Fees Payable Under the Act

	$
For recording conveyances, bills of sale, assignments, transfers, agreements, change of name, and other documents affecting title: For each lease in the document	5.00
For recording a Notice to Group, for each lease in the notice	5.00
For all copies or extracts from any documents, per page	.50
For filing a document, including power of attorney	5.00
For filing Letters Probate or Letters of Administration	5.00
For certifying documents	5.00
For each set of serially numbered metal identification tags	.50
Application fee, lease	10.00
Application fee, lease, extension	10.00
For late payment of rental, for every $50 rental payable	10.00

Every serious placer miner should obtain a copy of the Placer Mining Act Regulation. No Free Miner is permitted to stake more than two Placer Mining Leases (PML's) in any one year for himself although he may act as an agent for someone else who holds a valid Free Miner's Certificate.
Placer miners are also required to fill out the following forms for various reasons:

1. Any Free Miner after having staked a Placer Mining Lease (PML) by law is required to fill out an Affadavit for Placer Lease (Form H) and turn the affadavit in to the local Gold Commissioner. A $10 Application Fee and a $50 annual rental fee should accompany the affadavit.

2. Any Free Miner after having obtained a valid Lease (PML) and wishing to mine the lease must fill out and submit to the local Gold Commissioner a Notice of Work on a Placer Lease (Placer Form 10-11). This form must be completed and submitted prior to commencement of work and again one week prior to cessation of work. This form goes to the District Inspector of Mines.

3. Any Free Miner after having worked his lease (PML) should submit the Affadavit on Application to Record Work (Form J). $250 assessment work is required each season in order to hold a lease (PML). The assessment work must be done and the form submitted along with the annual rental fee of $50. If the assessment work is not done or this form not submitted a fee of $250 may be paid in lieu of assessment work. This is an important form and should always be completed on time.

Below is the list of towns and cities in British Columbia where regional maps, Free Miner's Certificates and the various forms may be obtained.

1. Alberni	16. Invermere	31. Prince Rupert
2. Ashcroft	17. Kamloops	32. Princeton
3. Atlin	18. Kaslo	33. Quesnel
4. Burns Lake	19. Kelowna	34. Revelstoke
5. Clinton	20. Kitimat	35. Rossland
6. Courtenay	21. Lillooet	36. Salmon Arm
7. Cranbrook	22. Merritt	37. Smithers
8. Creston	23. Nanaimo	38. Stewart
9. Duncan	24. Nelson	39. Telegraph Creek
10. Fernie	25. New Westminster	40. Terrace
11. Fort Nelson	26. Oliver	41. Vancouver
12. Fort St. John	27. Penticton	42. Vanderhoof
13. Ganges	28. Pouce Coupe	43. Vernon
14. Golden	29. Powell River	44. Williams Lake
15. Grand Forks	30. Prince George	45. Wells
		46. Victoria*

The next few pages have been devoted to the listing of a number of placer creeks, rivers and bars in various parts of the province. Although the list includes more than 400 spots there are about 200 more creeks of lesser importance which could have been included.

The creeks, rivers, gulches and bars are listed by regions and most of the great producers have been included.

It should be borne in mind that prospecting for placer gold creeks, rivers, ancient channels and so on, should be restricted to the historic gold districts. There have only been a handful of new discoveries made in the last three-quarters of a century and nearly all of these, except for a few in the northern part of the province, like Squaw Creek, have been found in known placer gold regions.

It should also be remembered that any Free Miner, although allowed access through a Placer Mining Lease (PML), cannot mine a lease belonging to another Free Miner without permission. Some old miners take exception to anyone even trespassing on their leases. Always check with the lease holder before travelling across his ground otherwise the lease holder may object, perhaps physically.

Below is the list of most of the placer gold creeks, rivers, bars and gulches in the province of British Columbia.

Atlin District

1. Bear Creek
2. Birch Creek
3. Blind Creek
4. Bonanza Creek
5. Boulder Creek
6. Bull Creek
7. Burdette Creek
8. Canyon Creek
9. Carvell Creek
10. Cracker Creek
11. Consolation Creek
12. Davenport Creek
13. Dixie Creek
14. Fourth of July Cr.
15. Fox Creek
16. Gold Run
17. Graham Creek
18. Lincoln Creek
19. McKee Creek
20. O'Donnel R.
21. Otter Creek
22. Pine Creek
23. Ruby Creek
24. Spruce Creek
25. Volcanic Creek
26. Wilson Creek
27. Wright Creek

Barkerville District (old name Cariboo)

1. Au Bau Creek
2. Alder Creek
3. Amador Creek
4. Anderson Creek
5. Antoine Creek
6. Antler Creek
7. Baker Creek
8. Baldhead Creek
9. Barr Creek
10. Beaver Creek
11. Beaver Pass Creek
12. Beggs Gulch
13. Berry Creek
14. Big Valley Creek
15. Big Wheel Flat
16. Black Bear Creek
17. Burns Creek
18. California Gulch
19. Campbell Creek
20. Canadian Creek
21. Canyon Creek
22. Captain Charlie Cr.
23. Cedar Creek
24. China Creek
25. Chisholm Creek
26. Coffee Creek
27. Conklin Creek
28. Cornish Creek
29. Cottonwood River
30. Coulter Creek
31. Cunningham Creek
32. Cunningham Pass Cr.
33. Davis Creek
34. Deadwood Creek
35. Devil's Canyon
36. Donovan Creek
37. Downie Pass Creek
38. Dragon Creek
39. Dunbar Flat
40. Eight Mile Lake
41. Emory Gulch
42. Empire Creek
43. Eureka Creek
44. Eureka Gulch
45. Fontaine Creek
46. Fort George Canyon
47. Four Mile Creek
48. French Creek
49. French Bar Creek
50. French Snowshoe Cr.
51. Gayton Creek
52. Goat River
53. Goose Creek
54. Government Creek
55. Grouse Creek
56. Grub Gulch
57. Hardscrabble Creek
58. Harvey Creek
59. Hixon Creek
60. Horsefly River
61. Houseman Creek
62. Jack of Clubs Cr.
63. Jawbone Creek
64. Kangaroo Creek
65. Keithley Creek
66. Last Chance Creek
67. Lightning Creek
68. Little Hixon Creek
69. Lowhee Creek
70. Little Swift River
71. Lowhee Creek
72. Martin Creek
73. Mary Creek
74. Mink Gulch
75. Montgomery Creek
76. Mosquito Creek
77. Morehead Creek
78. Mostique Creek
79. Mustang Creek
80. McArthur Gulch
81. McCallum Creek
82. Nelson Creek
83. New Creek
84. Nugget Gulch
85. Oregon Gulch
86. Perkins Gulch
87. Peters Creek
88. Pine Creek
89. Poquette Creek
90. Quesnel River
91. Red Gulch
92. Roses Gulch
93. Rouchon Creek
94. Sawmill Flat
95. Shepherd Creek
96. Slade Creek
97. Slough Creek
98. Snowshoe Creek
99. Sovereign Creek
100. Spanish Creek
101. Stevens Gulch
102. Stouts Gulch
103. Sugar Creek
104. Summit Creek
105. Swift River
106. Terry Creek
107. Timon Creek
108. Valley Creek
109. Van Winkle Creek
110. Walker Gulch
111. Williams Creek
112. West Road River
113. Willow River
114. Wormald Creek

Cherry Creek District (Okanagan)

1. Harris Creek
2. Lambly Creek
3. Mission Creek
4. Monashee Creek
5. Shuswap River
6. Trout Creek
7. Whiteman Creek

Dease District (Cassiar)

1. Alice Shea Creek
2. Barrington River
3. Cave Creek
4. Chutine River
5. Clear Creek
6. Dease Creek
7. Defot Creek
8. Dome Creek
9. Gold Pan Creek
10. McDame Creek
11. Mosquito Creek
12. Palmer Creek
13. Quartz Creek
14. Rosella Creek
15. Snow Creek
16. Stikine River
17. Thibert Creek
18. Trout Creek
19. Turnagain River
20. Wheaton Creek

French Creek District (Big Bend)

1. Carnes Creek
2. Columbia River
3. Downie Creek
4. French Creek
5. Goldstream River
6. McCulloch Creek
7. Kirbyville Cr.
8. Old Camp Creek

Fraser River (Fraser) and Tributaries

1. Alexander Creek
2. Bridge River
3. Cadwallader Creek
4. Cayoosh Creek
5. Churn Creek
6. Coquihalla River
7. Eldorado Creek
8. Gun Creek
9. Hurley River
10. Lillooet River
11. McGillivray Creek
12. Siwash Creek
13. Stirrup Creek

The Bars of the Fraser

1. Alfred Bar
2. American Bar
3. Angel's Bar
4. Big Bar
5. Bluenose Bar
6. Boothroyd's Flat
7. Boston Bar
8. Brady's Bar
9. Canadian Bar
10. Casey Bar
11. Chapman's Bar
12. China Bar (two)
13. China Flat
14. Cisco Bar
15. Clark's Riffle
16. Cornish Bar
17. Cross Bar
18. Dancing Bill's Bar
19. Davis Bar
20. Day's Bar
21. Deadwood Bar
22. Dutchman Bar
23. Eagle Bar
24. Emory Bar
25. Express Bar
26. Fargo's Bar
27. Fifty Four Forty B.
28. Foggarty's Bar
29. Fort Yale Bar
30. Foster's Bar
31. French Bar
32. Haskell's Bar
33. Hill's Bar
34. Horsebeef Bar
35. Hudson Bar
36. Humbug Bar
37. Island Bar
38. Kanaka Bar
39. Kennedy Bar
40. Lower Mormon Bar
41. Madison Bar
42. Maria Bar
43. McKeen's Bar
44. McMillan's Bar
45. McRae's Bar
46. Murderer's Bar
47. Murriner's Bar
48. New Brunswick Bar
49. New York Bar
50. Nicaragua Bar
51. Norman Bar
52. North Bend
53. Ohio Bar
54. Pike's Riffle
55. Posey Bar
56. Poverty Bar
57. Prince Albert
58. Prospect Bar
59. Puget Sound Bar
60. Rancheria Bar
61. Reed's Point
62. Rich Bar
63. Robinson Bar
64. Rocky Bar
65. Rose's Bar
66. Rough's Flat
67. Sacramento Bar
68. Sailor's Bar
69. Salmon River B.
70. Santa Clara Bar
71. Sawmill Riffle
72. Seabird Bar
73. Siwash Bar
74. Skuzzick Bar
75. Spuzzum Bar
76. Strangler's Bar
77. Strawberry Is.
78. Surprise Bar
79. Swan's Bar
80. Tehama Bar
81. Texas Bar
82. Trafalgar Bar
83. Trinity Bar
84. Union Bar
85. Upper Mormon B.
86. Van Winkle Bar
87. Victoria Bar
88. Ward's Bar
89. Washington Bar
90. Wellington Bar
91. Yankee Doodle F.
92. Yankee Flat

Leech and Loss River Areas (Vancouver Island)

1. Bedwell River
2. China Creek
3. Gordon River
4. Leech River
5. Loss River
6. San Juan River
7. Sombrio River
8. Sooke River
9. Zeballos River

Manson Creek and Ingenike Areas (Omineca)

1. Attichika Creek
2. Black Jack Gulch
3. Elmore Gulch
4. Finlay River
5. Germansen River
6. Harrison River
7. Ingenika River
8. Kenny Creek
9. Kildare Gulch
10. Little McLeod River
11. Lost Creek
12. Manson River
13. McConnell Creek
14. McLeod River
15. Nation River
16. Omineca River
17. Parsnip River
18. Philip Creek
19. Quartz Creek
20. Rainbow Creek
21. Silver Creek
22. Slate Creek
23. Tom Creek
24. Vital Creek
25. Wrede Creek

Moyie River and Vowell Creek Areas (East Kootenay)

1. Boulder Creek
2. Bull River
3. Canon Creek
4. Dutch Creek
5. Findlay Creek
6. Gold Creek
7. Moyie River
8. Palmer Bar Creek
9. Perry Creek
10. Quartz Creek
11. Toby Creek
12. Weaver Creek
13. Vowell Creek
14. Wildhorse River

Pend d'Oreille Area (West Kootenay)

1. Erie Creek
2. Forty-Nine Creek
3. Hall Creek
4. Lardeau Creek
5. Lardeau River
6. Lemon Creek
7. Pend d'Oreille R.
8. Rover Creek
9. Salmo River

Rock Creek Area (Boundary Country)

1. Baker Creek
2. Boundary Creek
3. Jolly Creek
4. July Creek
5. May Creek
6. McKinney Creek
7. Pass Creek
8. Rock Creek
9. Skeff Creek
10. West Kettle R.

Sowchea Creek Area

1. Dog Creek
2. Nechalo River
3. Sowchea Creek

Terrace Area

1. Chindemash Creek
2. Douglas Creek
3. Fiddler Creek
4. Gold Creek
5. Jimmay Creek
6. Kleanza Creek
7. Lorne Creek
8. Phillips Creek
9. Porcupine Creek
10. Sibola Creek
11. Twelve Mile Creek

Tulameen Area (Similkameen)

1. Britton Creek
2. Champion Creek
3. Collins Gulch
4. Granite Creek
5. Hayes Creek
6. Hines Creek
7. Lawless Creek
8. Lockie Creek
9. Manion Creek
10. Newton Creek
11. Olivine Creek
12. Similkameen River
13. Tulameen River
14. Whipsaw Creek

Miscellaneous Placer Creek and Rivers in other areas

1. Bob Creek (south of Houston, B.C.)
2. Buck Creek (south of Houston, B.C.)
3. Chilcotin River (west of Williams Lake, B.C.)
4. Jamieson Creek (north of Kamloops, B.C.)
5. Louis Creek (north of Kamloops, B.C.)
6. Mitchell Creek (north of Prince Rupert, B.C.)
7. Peace River (near Ft. St. John, B. C.)
8. Scotch Creek (north of Salmon Arm, B.C.)
9. Sulphurets Creek (north of Prince Rupert, B.C.)
10. Tranquille River (west of Kamloops, B.C.)
11. Unuk River (north of Prince Rupert, B.C.)

THE NUGGETS

Listed below are a number of the larger nuggets which have been found in the province from 1858 to the present. By necessity this list is incomplete as it is common knowledge that many of the larger nuggets recovered were not recorded, especially by the Chinese miners who were always reluctant to disclose good finds. In most instances the precise weight is given, in cases where the approximate weight is given it is marked with an asterisk.

Weight	Creek	District	Year	Locator
85 oz. 5 dwt.*	Spruce	Atlin	1899	West
73 oz.	Birch	Atlin	1913	
73 oz.*	McDame	Cassiar	1877	Freeman
52 oz. 15 dwt.	Alice Shea	Cassiar	1937	Shea
50 oz. 5 dwt.*	Boulder	Similkameen	1887	Unknown Chinese
50 oz.*	Dease	Cassiar	1875	Unknown
48 oz. 12 dwt.	Pine	Atlin	1925	
47 oz. 13 dwt.	Ruby	Atlin	1931	
46 oz. 5 dwt.	Squaw	Atlin	1936	
45 oz.*	Defot	Cassiar	1878	Unknown
44 oz. 3 dwt.	Spruce	Atlin	1936	Lykergaard
40 oz.*	Dease	Cassiar	1874	Unknown
36 oz. 10 dwt.	Spruce	Atlin	1902	Unknown
36 oz. 5 dwt.	Wild Horse	East Kootenay	1864	Reynolds
32 oz.*	Bridge R.	Fraser		Unknown
31 oz. 1 dwt.	Pine	Atlin	1899	Unknown
30 oz. 1 dwt.	Lightning	Cariboo	1864	Unknown
30 oz.*	Spruce	Atlin		Unknown
28 oz. 15 dwt.	McKee	Atlin	1901	Unknown
25 oz. ½ dwt.	Wright	Atlin	1899	Unknown
24 oz.*	Bear	Similkameen	1886	Unknown
24 oz.*	Germansen	Omineca	1934	

XXII

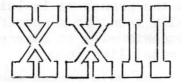

GLOSSARY

Some historic and modern words, terms and
phrases in common usage in placer mining.

Alloy - Probably derived from the French "a la loi," a mixture of two or more metals. An alloy is usually made for a specific reason, such as to give hardness to a metal or occasionally to debase a valuable metal such as gold with a less valuable metal like copper.

Apron - The apron is a part of the gold rocker and is located under the tray. It is constructed with blanket riffles on a frame designed to trap the gold, which passes through the punched holes of the tray. The apron is an integral part of a rocker.

Amalgamation - This is a process in which mercury or quicksilver is amalgamated with another substance, usually gold in the fine state when it is mixed with black-sand. Mercury, having a natural affinity for gold picks it up and amalgamates it. Later the mercury is burned off leaving only a gold "button."

Assay - It placer mining terminology this term means an analysis of gold bearing gravels to determine the values contained therein.

Bar - A bar is a projection of sand or gravel into a creek or river. The bars of certain rivers, like the Fraser, were often gold bearing. Hill's Bar, several miles south of Yale was the richest placer gold bar in the province. It yielded perhaps three tons of gold.

Barren - This term is generally used to describe an area, stream or dirt which contains no gold.

Bedrock - This is an impervious layer upon which placer gold settles. It is what every experienced placer man looks for. See "Chapter II" entitled "Bedrock" for details.

Benches - A term used to describe a flat above a creek or river. They are sometimes gold-bearing and occasionally richer than the actual bed of the creek or river.

Blacksand - This material invariably occurs with placer gold and may make up most of the concentrate in the gold pan. Blacksand is usually composed of magnetite which may be removed from the pan by the use of a magnet. Black sand is an indicator of gold, if it is not present in an area which is being tested, it is unlikely that placer gold exists there.

Bonanza - This term is derived from a Spanish word which means prosperity. The miners frequently used this word when referring to an exceptionally rich creek or diggings. Hence the phrase, "Bonanza Creek," indicated the richest of placer streams.

Bullion - An ingot of gold or silver which has been obtained by refining and melting down the crude or natural metal. Seldom pure in the old days, it was often shipped, for convenience, in this form.

Celestials - Another expression which emanated from the California goldfields and was the usual word used to describe the Chinese miners of that state. This term, often used contemptuously, was carried northward by the Forty-Niners in 1858. The term came from "The Celestial Empire," a name commonly used to describe China at that time. Sometimes puzzling to the uninitiated, this word frequently occurs in diaries, letters and newspaper reports from British Columbia which are dated prior to 1900.

China Diggings - A phrase which also originated in the Golden State and was subsequently used in nearly all of the goldfields in British Columbia to describe ground which was considered unprofitable by white standards.

The Chinese, however, often worked placer creeks which had been either abandoned or bypassed by their white counterparts and regarded by the latter as poor diggings. It was later discovered that some of the "China Diggings," especially in the Cariboo, Tulameen and the Boundary Country were vastly richer than had been suspected, a fact which the shrewd and taciturn Chinese had wisely not disclosed to the white miners.

Claim - An area which has been legally let to a Free Miner to work for a specified period of time. Most old miners stake leases, which are larger in area, rather than claims but still refer to their leases as "claims." In creek diggings a claim is normally two hundred and fifty feet long by one thousand feet wide.

Claim Jumping - Along with sluice-box robbing and highgrading, this was considered the most serious crime in the mining camps of the old West. This phrase evidently originated in the United States, supposedly in the gold-fields of California, and later gained common usage throughout the entire West. "Claim jumping" was the act of one individual who illegally restaked or "jumped" a claim which had previously been legally staked by another miner. Often bloody and occasionally deadly affrays arose from disputes concerning claim jumping. In the early records from Yale, Hope, Boston Bar, Lytton and other old gold towns along the Fraser in the old days, there are numerous references to fights, shootings and murders, a direct result of this offence.

Clean-up - This is a term used to describe the procedure of retrieving gold after the gold-bearing gravels have been washed. Various types of sluices were used during the washing and the clean-up entailed a careful cleaning of the riffles, apron or any other apparatus used to catch or trap the gold. One of the most important and interesting procedures in placer mining.

Coarse Gold - Gold which is too large to pass through a 10 mesh screen is considered "coarse gold." Most of the gold of this type tends to be rough-edged and usually includes nuggets of varying sizes. Coarse gold usually brings a premium price.

Colours - A term used to describe particles of gold, often mere specks, flakes or dust. "Colours" in the pan, sluice or rocker are indicative of gold-bearing ground. The more numerous and larger the colours, the more promising the ground. Good prospectors always keep a sharp eye out for this infallible indicator.

Concentrates - This is the accumulated material or residue remaining in the pan, sluicebox or rocker after washing. The majority of the material is blacksand, although it may include garnets, ironstone, native silver and other impurities. In rare instances, as in the Similkameen-Tulameen platinum may be present along with the gold. The residue is panned down to obtain the "noble" metals like gold, platinum and electrum.

Crevice - This is a split or crack in the bedrock into which placer gold has often gravitated and remained. Such fissures were meticulously mined by experienced placer men. Some crevices in the Cariboo yielded as much as 50 pounds troy of gold.

Dead Work - This is a phrase used to describe the labour involved when driving towards paydirt. Dead-work is usually expensive and laborious, especially when the overburden was deep and barren.

Deposit - This word is usually used to denote a mass of gravel or material which contains some gold.

Diggings - An old term long used in the West to describe an area which was being actively mined. "Dry" diggings were bench diggings, and "wet" diggings were creek deposits.

Discovery Claim - This was the first claim on a newly discovered placer creek. The discoverer was allowed to stake a "Discovery Claim" which was legally larger than any subsequent claims staked on the same stream. In the Yukon, North-West Territories and even Atlin, other claims were measured according to the Discovery Claim, thus giving rise to names like "36 Below" and "24 Above," meaning, of course, their position above or below the first or "Discovery" claim.

Dolly - A seldom used word used to describe a rocker.

Dragline - This is an intergal part of a dragline dredge, the cable or line upon which the bucket runs or swings during operation.

Dredge - This is a term used to describe a machine, usually located on a floating barge, which is employed to raise gold-bearing gravels from the river or creek floor by utilizing mechanical scoops, buckets, suction or other methods. The paydirt was lifted and ultimately processed by the apparatus aboard the dredge. A variety of dredges were used all through the gold producing regions of the province. A rather interesting observation is that dredges originated, not in North America, but rather in New Zealand; evolving from a primitive spoon dredge to a current wheel dredge and eventually into a complete and self-contained outfit. By 1890 there were a number of dredges in the Otago region of that country. The idea caught on in North America and were especially successful in parts of the Yukon but rarely in British Columbia. Today numerous prospectors are using small portable dredges like those made by outfits like Keene Engineering of California. Technically illegal for mining, they are used for rather extensive testing but should not be used in rivers or creeks that have extensive runs of salmon or trout.

Drifting - This simply means horizontal tunneling into a bank in order to reach paydirt or bedrock or to follow a promising lead. After shallow and easily worked deposits were exhausted, drifting was later resorted to if the paydirt was considered rich enough to warrant the expense. An expensive and time-consuming method of mining.

Dust - In mining parlance this term refers to raw placer gold which is made up of extremely fine flakes or "dust," hence the origin of this old term which is still used occasionally in parts of the province.

El Dorado - Derived from the Spanish which, loosely translated, means, "the golden place," a mythical country in South America supposedly very rich in gold and long sought by early Spanish explorers like DeSoto and Balboa. Eventually this term came to mean any region which was rich in gold. Thus an "El Dorado" creek was an exceptionally productive placer stream. Williams, Lightning, Pine, Spruce, Granite, Dease, Wild Horse, McDame and other rich creeks were all considered El Dorado creeks.

Electrum - A strange amalgam of silver and gold which is found on only a few placer creeks in British Columbia. Usually confused with platinum or native silver, it has a silvery tone with a yellowish tinge. It is a relatively hard metal found on Poquette Creek in the Cariboo and on the Similkameen River in the Tulameen district.

Fine Gold - This term is used to describe gold which can pass through a 40 mesh screen. Placer gold falling into this category is usually called "dust" or "flour" gold.

Fineness - This word relates to the relative purity of gold, that is, the ratio of gold to silver in placer gold. The gold from every placer gold stream in the province is gauged by its fineness. The range of fineness is astonishing; from 712 fine for Monashee Creek near Vernon to almost 970 fine, which means 970 parts gold per 1000, from the Goat River. The average fineness from over 170 streams in the province is 861, meaning that it average 86.1% pure gold. Placer gold is, of course, an alloy of both gold and silver. Pure placer gold does not exist naturally.

Flour Gold - Sometimes called "dust," this type of gold usually occurs on river bars. The Fraser, Quesnel, Bridge, Cottonwood, Stikine, Peace, Similkameen and many other rivers in the province were, and remain, the major sources of this type of gold.

Fool's Gold - This is miner's jargon for any material which looks like or resembles gold and is taken for the real thing by the inexperienced. The most common substance taken for gold by the uninitiated is mica. It is found in most of the gold-bearing creeks of the West. Mica glitters in the pan in sunlight but its properties are considerably removed from gold - it is very light and splits easily with a knife blade. Any close examination will readily prove it worthless.

Fraction - This is a mining word which describes an area lying between two claims. Fractions were staked when one of the claims was found to be too long or beyond their legal limits. The celebrated Cariboo prospector called "Twelve Foot" Davis received his sobriquet after he staked a 12' fraction on famous Williams Creek between two other claims. The fraction he staked ultimately yielded almost $950,000 in gold at today's price.

Free Miner - Any individual who is 18 years of age or more and who holds a Free Miner's Certificate.

Giant - A giant is a special type of monitor used in hydraulicking. The "giant" was used to direct water under pressure to break down the gravel banks so that the gravel could be sluiced to recover the gold.

Gold Rush - Also known as a "stampede." This is an old term which came into common use in California and later all through the West. It is used to describe any sudden or mass movement of miners into a district where gold was discovered. This phenomenon occurred in California, Australia, the Klondike and the Cariboo in the 19th century.

Gradient - This term refers to the dip or grade of a stream or a sluice-box. A good gradient ennabled a miner to bring water to an operation, a poor gradient made mining, especially sluicing difficult and expensive.

Grains - This usually refers to small particles of gold or to the small weights used in the Troy Weight system. Under that system a total of 24 grains equals 1 pennyweight. As there are 20 pennyweights to the ounce, 480 grains would also equal one ounce Troy.

Grizzly - A device used to keep rocks or boulders out of a sluice-box. A grizzly is a heavy screen set up at the head of a sluice (where the dirt is dumped), at an angle so that all oversize material, like rocks, will roll off.

Ground Sluicing - The use of ground water to wash away overburden. The water was usually diverted to a desired place and turned in to wash off the overburden to get to the "pay" gravels underneath.

Hand - This old term simply means "miner." Thus the phrase "15 per day per hand," meant $15 per day per miner." Its origin is obscure.

Hardpan - This is another name for "false bedrock." Sometimes hardpan looked like true bedrock and acted like it. Quite often placer gold is found lying directing on this layer but in other instances the gold has penetrated it and lies on true bedrock.

Hidden Values - In miners' terminology this refers to the unseen values usually found in blacksand concentrates. These values are occasionally very misleading because there are few extractive processes which can, at least inexpensively, recover all the hidden values. A term which is misleading and misused.

Hydraulic - This is a word used to describe a common method of mining in which water under pressure is used to cut away banks of gold-bearing gravels or overburden. Water is brought to the operation with a great enough "head" (or pressure) and discharged into a pipeline, at the end of which is a nozzle called a "monitor" or "giant." By using the water pressure provided the overburden is cut away to expose the gold-bearing gravels which are then sluiced.

Ironstone - This is the "indicator" stone. It is a heavy, rounded rock usually small in size, blackish in colour with sometimes a bluish or a reddish oxidization. On more than two-thirds of the placer gold creeks in the province "ironstone" is found in the same run as gold. The good prospector is always on the lookout for ironstone because when he finds it he knows that gold is near at hand.

Jade - A semi-precious stone found in many places along the Fraser and Bridge rivers and in northern British Columbia. In the early years of mining along the Fraser it is rumoured that the Chinese miners, aware of the value of this stone, shipped great quantities of it to China.

John - A derogatory term used to designate the Chinese miner. This word originated in California in the 1850s and was carried north by miners from the Golden State. Fortunately, it has fallen into disuse.

Junction - This refers to the confluence or meeting point of streams or rivers. Where they come together.

Karat - This word is used to describe the purity of gold. 24 karats is pure gold, 21 karats is 21/24ths pure. Thus the letters "10k" on a gold ring would indicate that the ring was only 10/24ths gold, the remainder consisting of an alloy, usually either copper or silver.

Lay - In miners' jargon this word is used to describe a working agreement between a lease holder and a miner working his lease. Under such an agreement, the miner leases the ground from the original holder and agrees to pay the former a percentage (usually from 10% to 20%) of the gold recovered. Most of these agreements were honoured by both parties. Today it is wise to have a written agreement.

Lead - This word is used to describe a "run" of gold which occurs on nearly all placer streams. It is usually a layer of gravel close to bedrock in which high values are encountered. Miners always attempt to follow the leads if they are rich. "Lost leads" are runs of gold which have pinched out and cannot be traced by miners.

Lease - A Lease in an area granted by the Gold Commissioner to a Free Miner who has properly staked and recorded the ground applied for. The size of a lease is 1000 meters by 500 meters and must be defined by a legal "initial" post and a legal "final" post and a location line. A Placer Mining Lease (PML) is usually granted for a period of 10 years, during which an annual rental fee of $50 must be paid and assessment work to the value of $250 must be done and filed each year.

Located - This word simply means that a miner has "staked" a certain area in order to mine the ground. An old term sometimes still used.

Lode - This word is used to describe the place of origin of the metal being mined. Hence the "lode" or starting place, was always searched for assiduously by prospectors in the hopes of finding "ore in place."

Low Grade - In mining terminology this means deposits of metal, either placer or lode, which contains values too low to mine except by large-scale methods. Hobson's celebrated "Bullion Mine" in the Cariboo was a low grade placer operation which was largely successful because of the large volume of gravel processed.

Mercury - An element called "quicksilver" by placer miners and used by them to recover gold from blacksand because of the peculiar affinity of this metal to amalgamate or combine with gold. Later, the gold in the "amalgam" (or mixture) was recovered by driving the mercury off, either by retorting or by putting the amalgam in a potato (which has been cut in half) wired together and baked over an open fire. Mercury should not be retorted by novices as the fumes are deadly.

Monitor - Another word for a "giant," essentially a brass nozzle used to direct water under high pressure in order to remove overburden or to break down gold-bearing gravels in order to sluice them. Monitors were used in hydraulic operations.

Motherlode - A term often misused. It is the original starting place, or origin, of a metal. A vein which contains the metal "in place."

Nugget - A word meaning a piece, lump or specimen of native gold. This word was probably derived from "nug," an archaic English word meaning "lump." It is used to describe any specimen of native gold valued at $1.00 or more at current prices. It is also used to describe pieces of native silver, platinum, electrum, copper and so on.

Old Channel - Miners use this phrase to describe any former or original course or channel of a creek or river. Considerable effort and expense is often expended in attempting to find ancient channels in placer gold regions as they sometimes contain very rich "runs" of gold.

Ounce a Day - A phrase much used in the early days of placer mining in the West. Diggings which yielded "an ounce a day" to the hand were rich diggings. When the returns dipped to less than this amount, the miners often moved on in search of other more lucrative ground. In the 1860s and 1870s "ounce a day" diggings were found in many regions of British

Columbia, including the Cariboo, Cassiar, Atlin, Similkameen, Big Bend and East Kootenay.

Overburden - This is ground which must be penetrated or removed to get to the paydirt. In many cases the overburden consisted of poor paying or barren gravels which covered a higher paying run of gold which lay on or close to bedrock. In placer mining overburden was often removed by hydraulicking.

Pan - This word has a dual meaning. It may be used to describe mining with a gold pan or it may be used simply when referring to a gold pan. To "pan" gravel means to wash the gravel in a gold pan to obtain the gold.

Pay - A word used to describe ground which is rich in placer gold. In other words, gold-bearing gravel which returns "wages" or better to the miner.

Paystreak - A peculiar phrase in mining parlance to describe the layer of gravel in which high values are obtained. In some creeks there may be several "paystreaks." Sometimes the word "run" is used instead.

Pennyweight - A measure used in Troy weight. 20 pennyweights equal 1 Troy ounce. There are 24 grains in 1 pennyweight.

Placer - This is a deposit of gravel which contains particles of gold or other valuable metals. Gold was, and still is, the most important mineral found in placers. This word was derived from the Spanish word meaning "sand bank."

Platinum - A valuable metal which occurs occasionally in placer gold deposits. Found in many areas in British Columbia in small amounts it occurs in quantity only in the Similkameen-Tulameen district in great amounts. In that district an estimated 20,000 ounces were recovered in the early days. It is silvery in colour and nearly as heavy as placer gold. Almost always fine-grained, nuggets in the province are rarely found. It is usually only 65% pure.

Pocket - A deposit where a heavy concentration of gold is found. This may occur in crevices, under large boulders or any other place where the force of water had deposited large quantities of gold.

Poke - A small leather bag used by prospectors in the early years to store and carry their gold. Usually about 5" to 6" in length and about 2" in width with a draw-string at the top. Used only occasionally now it has been replaced by less romantic containers.

Poor Man's Diggings - A misleading phrase in some respects because it is a phrase which actually describes placer gold deposits or diggings which were shallow and could be worked by a "poor man" for a profit. "Poor man's diggings" were diligently sought by prospectors who could mine them without capital and make a stake.

Pot Hole - A word used to describe a depression in the bed-rock of a creek or river. Highly over-rated because they seldom contain appreciable amounts of gold because any gold deposited in them is ground fine by water action and rocks and washed back into the stream.

Production - A term used to describe the total yield or output of gold from a given locality.

Types of riffles - Courtesy Bulletin No. 15 published by the British Columbia Department of Mines in 1942.

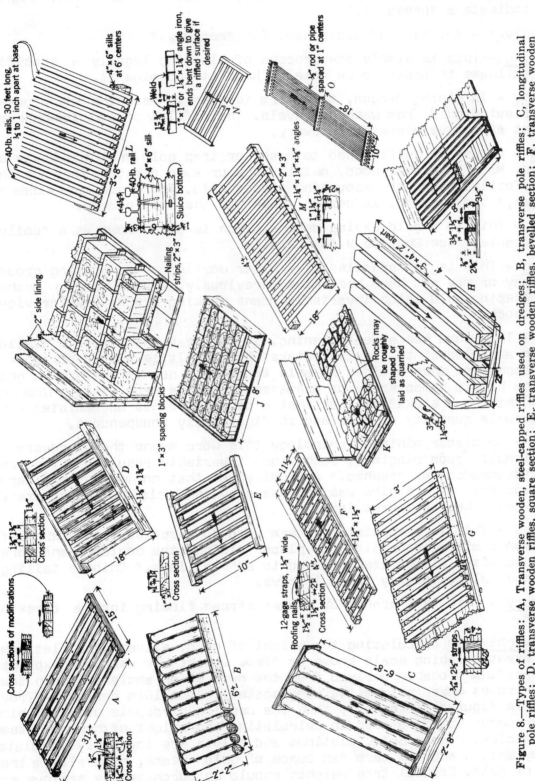

Figure 8.—Types of riffles: A, Transverse wooden, steel-capped riffles used on dredges; B, transverse pole riffles; C, longitudinal pole riffles; D, transverse wooden riffles, square section; E, transverse wooden riffles, bevelled section; F, transverse wooden riffle, steel-capped, inclined section; G, transverse wooden riffles, steel-clad, with overhang; H, longitudinal wooden riffles capped with cast-iron plates; I, wooden-block riffles for large sluices; J, wooden-block riffles for undercurrents; K, stone riffles; L, longitudinal rail riffles on wooden sills; M, transverse angle-iron riffles; N, transverse angle-iron riffles with top tilted upward; O, longitudinal riffles made of iron pipe; P, transverse cast-iron riffles used in undercurrents.

<u>Prospecting</u> - The act of searching for a "prospect." The prospector is actively engaged in attempting to find a place where profitable mining can be carried on. He looks for "colours," "float" or any other signs which indicate a "prospect."

<u>Quicksilver</u> - Another and older name for "mercury."

<u>Recording</u> - This is simply the process of claiming legally a specific claim or lease in order to be able to hold it and mine it.

<u>Recovery</u> - In mining jargon, this term is used to describe the process of retrieving gold from washed gravels. The riffles of a sluice-box are the most effective means of recovery.

<u>Riffle</u> - A type of baffle used to catch or trap gold in sluice-boxes or rockers. Made of either wood, metal, rock or even plastic, they are the most effective means of recovering placer gold. There are many kinds of "riffles," block, pole, ladder or cross are the most common.

<u>Rocker</u> - This is a gold saving device which is also known as a "dolly" or a "cradle." See Chapter V for details.

<u>Sniping</u> - This is the practise of a miner working or re-working ground which may or may not have been mined previously. A fascinating method of recovering gold which invariably means working cracks and crevices in bed-rock.

<u>Stake</u> - This word has a dual meaning. It may mean the action of placing tags on a claimpost to legally "stake" ground. It is also used to describe occasions when a miner is able to amass a quantity of placer gold to allow him to temporarily or premanently retire from mining. Thus the phrase "making a stake" implies that a prospector has accumulated some considerable quantity of gold and is financially independent.

<u>Strike</u> - In placer mining terminology this word means the discovery of exceptionally good diggings. Such finds invariably resulted in the area being "stampeded" or "rushed." An oddity was that no matter how carefully the news of a strike was supressed by the original discoverers, it was never kept a secret long.

<u>Tailings</u> - This is a specialized term used to describe the residue left over from a mining operation. In placer mining, the boulders and rocks discarded after mining are referred to as "tailings." Chinese tailings are almost always neatly piled in rows.

<u>Tributary</u> - This is a branch or feeder stream flowing into a creek or a river.

<u>Troy Weight</u> - In calculating the weight of gold, silver and platinum, a different weighing scale known as "Troy weight" is used. The expression "Troy" was probably derived from the name of an ancient French town called Troyes where goldsmiths congregated in the 16th century. "Troy" weight is figured differently than the usual avoirdupois weight, which is the common standard used in calculating the weight of ordinary items and articles. Placer gold, platinum and silver are invaribly calculated in Troy Weight and the term "an ounce of gold" means, naturally, a troy ounce of gold. Special troy weights should be purchased by serious and dedicated placer miners when weighing, selling or buying placer gold.

The Troy Weights			Avoirdupois Weights		
24 grains	=	1 pennyweight	437½ grains	=	1 ounce
480 grains	=	20 pennyweights	7000 grains	=	16 ounces
20 pennyweights	=	1 troy ounce	16 ounces	=	1 pound
12 troy ounces	=	1 troy pound			
5760 grains	=	1 troy pound or 12 troy ounces			

Values - This term is used to describe the relative worth of placer gold contained in gold-bearing gravels. It may also include the value of other precious metals, like platinum, which would increase the value.

Virgin Ground - This term refers to any gold-bearing ground which has not been mined. In the early years prospectors were always looking for "virgin" creeks or ground. Since 1900 only half a dozen "Virgin" gold creeks have been discovered. There are isolated and deep spots in most of the placer districts where virgin ground has yet to be mined but most of it is too expensive to mine. Lightning Creek is a typical example but the problems there and elsewhere make it too expensive to mine the ground profitably.

Washing - This is an expression which describes the action of panning or sluicing gold-bearing gravels to recover the gold contained therein. The "washing" of gravels results in running off the worthless material leaving only the precious metals behind.

Waste - Any material which is considered valueless is commonly referred to as "waste." Tailings, black sand and barren gravels (including rocks and boulders) would all come under this heading.

Weathered - A much used term which means "worn." This term is generally used when referring to well worn bedrock. Glacial or water action on the surface of the rock usually brought about this condition. In the Cariboo certain weathered rock referred to as "cowstongues" were an indicator of gold close at hand and experienced miners there always watch for them.

Wheel - This may refer to a variety of wheeled devices used by the placer men, especially in the early days. Overshot wheels, undershot wheels and Cornish wheels and current wheels were just a few of the wheels used to raise water or provide water for mining.

Wing-dam - This was a type of dam build into the stream or river in order to be able to effectively mine shallow bedrock. The Chinese were skilled wing-dammers. The wing-dam was seldom built straight out in the creek or river but rather at an angle (downstream slightly) so that the current of the river would not break the wing-dam. Seldom used today, it was a favourite way of mining in the 19th century. Rivers like the Wild Horse, the Quesnel and the Similkameen were all wing-dammed by the Chinese miners of the 1860s and 1870s who recovered astonishing amounts of placer gold from their efforts.

Yield - This term is used to describe the output or production of placer gold from a given operation. A high "yield" would mean that the recovery of precious metals was worthwhile. Some of the yield was in fine gold or platinum which sold at less than the going rate. Today a yield which is primarily in coarse gold and nuggets fetches a higher premium because the nuggets sell for much more than fine gold because of their collector's or specimen value.

HISTORY TITLES BY HANCOCK HOUSE

**Barkerville —
The Town That Gold Built**
Lorraine Harris

**Fraser Canyon — From
Cariboo Road to Super Highway**
Lorraine Harris

Gold Along the Fraser
Lorraine Harris

Manning Park
Lorraine Harris

British Columbia Railway
Lorraine Harris

**Walhachin —
Catastrophe or Camelot?**
Joan Weir

Powell Lake
Carla Mobley

Gold Panning in British Columbia
N. L. Barlee

Gold Creeks and Ghost Towns
N. L. Barlee

**Similkameen — The Gold and Ghost
Towns of the Hope-Princeton Area**
N. L. Barlee

**Lost Mines — The Historic Treasures
of British Columbia**
N. L. Barlee

Gold! Gold!
Joseph Petralia

**Backroad Adventures through
Interior B.C.**
Donovan Clemson

Old Wooden Buildings
Donovan Clemson

Living With Logs
Donovan Clemson

Craigmont Story
Murphy Shewchuk

Fur, Gold and Opals
Murphy Shewchuk

B.C. Recalled
Derek Pethick

Vancouver Recalled
Derek Pethick

Mighty Mackenzie
Lyn Hancock

Mackenzie Yesterday and Beyond
Alfred P. Aquilina

Fishing in B.C.
Forrester and Forrester

Mining in B.C.
G. W. Taylor

Trucking in B.C.
Andy Craig

Logging in B.C.
Ed Gould

Ranching in Western Canada
Ed Gould

Oil in Canada
Ed Gould

Big Timber, Big Man
Carol Lind

Nahanni
Dick Turner

Wings of the North
Dick Turner

Ralph Edwards of Lonesome Lake
Ed Gould

Ruffles in my Longjohns
Isabel Edwards

Fogswamp
Trudy Turner

Northern Man
Jim Martin

Novice in the North
Jim Robinson

Alaska Calls
Virginia Neely

Ho for the Klondike
G. Miller